The Pecan

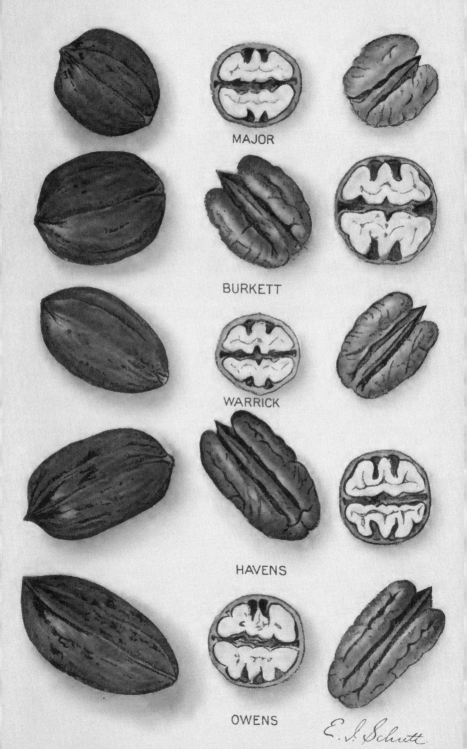

MAJOR

BURKETT

WARRICK

HAVENS

OWENS

E. I. Schutt.

MAJOR, BURKETT, WARRICK, HAVENS, AND OWENS PECANS.

A HISTORY OF AMERICA'S NATIVE NUT

BY JAMES MCWILLIAMS

University of Texas Press
AUSTIN

Requests for permission to reproduce material from this work
should be sent to:
Permissions
University of Texas Press
P.O. Box 7819
Austin, TX 78713-7819
http://utpress.utexas.edu/index.php/rp-form

⊗ The paper used in this book meets the minimum requirements
of ANSI/NISO Z39.48-1992 (R1997) (Permanence of Paper).

LIBRARY OF CONGRESS CATALOGING-IN-PUBLICATION DATA
McWilliams, James E.
The pecan : a history of America's native nut / by James McWilliams.
— First edition.
pages   cm
Includes bibliographical references and index.
ISBN 978-0-292-74916-0 (cloth : alk. paper)
1. Pecan. 2. Pecan industry. I. Title.
SB401.P4M39 2013
634'.52—dc23   2013002834

doi:10.7560/749160

*pp. ii and 156: U.S. Department of Agriculture Pomological Watercolor Collection.
Rare and Special Collections, National Agricultural Library, Beltsville, MD 20705.*

For Marvin Harris, with gratitude

Question: Please settle a dispute. We can't agree on the pronunciation of pecan.
Answer: First choice: p-KAHN. Second choice, heard usually in the Northern and Eastern states, pee-KAN.

FRANK COLBY, *LOS ANGELES TIMES*,
MARCH 25, 1950

The pecan is a nut originally 100 percent American, which has been allowed to remain 95 percent American. Most of the tasty new foods Europeans discovered in America eventually made their way around the world, some quickly, some slowly, but the United States has been left in almost complete possession of the pecan.

WAVERLY ROOT, *LOS ANGELES TIMES*,
OCTOBER 19, 1978

CONTENTS

PREFACE

I decided to write about the pecan tree for purely personal reasons. I have no professional training in trees or nuts. I'm not a scientist. My botany knowledge derives mainly from popular writing and amateurish reading of textbooks. I'm even relatively new to the field of environmental history, the discipline that I sometimes call home. So, the inevitable question: why write a book on the history of pecans?

A wild pecan tree grows directly through the middle of my back deck in Austin, Texas. It presents itself to the world every day, proudly and without fail. The deck is built around it. The crown of the stately fifty-foot tree hovers above my office like a tilted umbrella. When it's masting—producing nuts—it peppers my metal roof with relentless pings, and crows, as if tipped off in advance, arrive en masse to crack into them. One afternoon, while sitting in my office reading Gilbert White's *The Natural History of Selborne* for a class I was teaching, with pecans peppering my roof, I had a sobering thought: I didn't know a damn thing about this tree. I'm generally fascinated by the natural world. Nonetheless, here was a specimen that I saw every day, heard hitting my roof about every other fall, and more than occasionally used as a food source. As far as my own knowledge was concerned, though, it may as well have been a boulder. In some basic sense, this seemed wrong.

Gilbert White, the author I was reading, would never have tolerated such ignorance. White was an English botanist and naturalist who spent much of the 1760s and 1770s observing the finest details of his own backyard. The natural world of the southern English town where he was born and raised, Selborne, served as his lifelong laboratory, the biodiverse context of his boundless curiosity. White dissected the habits and history of every plant, animal, stream, and pond in the vicinity. No detail escaped his razor-sharp attention and no description seemed to evade his pen. He reveled in the strange beauty of the natural mysteries around him, mysteries that were, for most people, hidden in plain sight. He brought those mysteries out of hiding with childlike enthusiasm, telling his stories with subtle humor and honesty. With humility, he was just looking. The results, without in any way intending to be, were dazzling.

Of course, Selborne had no pecan trees, and let it now be said, I'm no Gilbert White. Indeed, not only did White never mention pecans, but it is likely the man never even saw one, wedded as he was to his windswept homeland. Nevertheless, his book, which celebrates deliberateness and patience in every paragraph, lent me inspiration. There's much to learn from White's distilled enthusiasm for the natural history of his own backyard. *The Natural History of Selborne* reminds us that the most timeless stories, and the most sublime discoveries, are often the ones lurking just beyond our narrowly trained frame of reference. This realization is what grabbed me and got me thinking, studying, and, alas, writing about the pecan tree. These writings—"scribblings" they would once have been called—initially took form as a file on my laptop called "Pecan Notes." After about a month of keeping these notes I had somehow, by whatever intuitive calculus leads to such a conclusion, determined that I was, somehow or other, writing a book.

As a writer with an almost obsessive interest in contemporary agricultural issues, I found the pecan intriguing for other reasons as well. Essentially, it came to fascinate me as a tree indigenous to the United States that in a remarkably short span of time (by agricultural standards) went from being primarily wild to being primarily domesticated. The nut that European settlers found in the seventeenth century, much less the nut that Native Americans found more than ten thousand years ago, is not the nut we know today. Human intervention has been diverse, involving everyone from hunter-gatherer opportunists to twenty-first-century agronomists. Collectively, the intervention has radically altered pecans to the point that the majority of them around today owe their existence to human "improvement."

Through this improvement, the pecan became one of the very few plants native to North America to evolve into a significant agricultural crop. The transition from wild to cultivated is ultimately what interests me—not, I should add, writing a comprehensive history of the pecan (which this book is decidedly not). This transformation from the wild to the sown is the driving theme of my book. It is a topic that bears directly upon nothing less important than the human quest to eat food. As I worked on tracing this narrative, it gradually hit me that to grasp this basic history of the pecan tree was to grasp a story that, in essence, was a fertile microcosm of the complex and productive—and sometimes power-hungry and dysfunctional—relationship that humans maintain with the plant kingdom. And in that, I soon learned, there was drama.

ACKNOWLEDGMENTS

*I would never have written this book were it not for the infectious pas-*sion for pecan trees demonstrated by my friend and Texas A&M entomologist Dr. Marvin Harris. I've dedicated this book, warts and all, to him because of his rare compassion for me, a historian trying to understand plant biology. Equally pivotal in nurturing this idea to life was Casey Kittrell, my editor at the University of Texas Press, who lent ceaseless encouragement (and micro-brew-drinking companionship) as this book slowly became a book. Further critical support came from my friend Carolle R. Morini, tireless archivist at the Boston Athenæum. The ongoing professional and moral support provided by my smartest friend in the world, Scott Gabriel Knowles, a historian of technology at Drexel University, was invaluable. Most important, as always, is my family, who, amazingly, astoundingly, flawlessly, passionately, somehow tolerate my unpredictable and all-too-isolating endeavors with humor, love, and understanding. Family, you are my taproot.

A Miami chief named Pacane, drawn by Henry Hamilton
sometime between 1776 and 1778. The name suggests the
central place of the pecan in Native American material culture
and personal identity. *Henry Hamilton drawings of North American scenes
and Native Americans: Guide. Houghton Library, Harvard College Library.*

Cracking the Nut

Here is an intriguing hypothesis: nuts may have made our prehuman ancestors smarter. Smarter because the nut forms in a shell and our hominid forebears had to think a bit about how to extract it. Thought led to innovation. Innovation to nutrition. Nutrition to greater intelligence. That's the idea, anyway. Granted, finding a stone flat enough to shatter a nut doesn't really qualify as unique cognition—apes do it all the time. But not unlike the way a seagull, after multiple attempts, finally figures out how high to soar before dropping the clam, it required trial and error. Smash the nut too fiercely, whack it in the wrong spot with the wrong rock, and shell shards splinter into the meat. Get it just right, though, with the right rock on the right seam with the right pressure, and you've just opened a new chapter in culinary history. When the first nut was cracked, the history of eating, it seems fair to say, changed significantly.[1]

We have no idea when or where it happened. No idea whatsoever who the first opposable-thumbed hominid was who successfully liberated a nut from its shell. However, it stands to reason that whenever it took place, life changed for the better. Prehuman and human history is marked by major transformations: the harnessing of fire, the domestication of wheat, irrigation, animal breeding, refrigeration, genetic modification, the advent of the Twinkie. Rarely included among these prehistoric and historic milestones is the simple act of cracking open a nut. This fundamental historical act, I submit, deserves its due. The cracked nut may not have profoundly altered the course of human events, but it played an important role in shaping material and economic life for hundreds of millions of people for hundreds and thousands of years.[2]

Of course, nuts didn't evolve shells to improve the minds of our prehistoric ancestry. On the contrary, a nut is a fruit with a single seed that's indehiscent—it does not open upon reaching maturity. Its hard exterior protects the seed (which is technically a one-seeded dry fruit) from the elements. The fact that we managed to break the nut's barrier and, over thousands of years, enjoy its fruit and, over the last hundred years, dictate the genetic course of its development doesn't mean that nuts lost and humans won. Nature, which is defined by unintended consequences, really doesn't follow that kind of logic. Plus, nature is ultimately too elusive and too powerful to assume a subservient role to a recent arrival such as the human, no matter how impressive his brain or how advanced his technologies.

When humans and plants enter into a relationship, a level of humility is forced upon us as we become integrated into unfamiliar natural processes. A mutually beneficial balance, never perfect, is the only way to ensure that the relationship— much less the plant itself—enjoys some semblance of longevity. For most of history, humans have responsibly propagated nuts. Nuts, in return, have generously, if more passively, improved the health of humans. They have thrived. We have thrived. How long this balance will persist into the future is, as we will see in the last chapter of this story, very much an open question, one we should probably be thinking about more seriously than we do.[3]

Pecan trees (*Carya illinoinensis*) have lent themselves especially well to a delicate symbiosis with humans. Pecans belong to the family Juglandaceae, the pollen of which first appeared in the late Cretaceous period, about 135 million years ago. About 80 million years later the phylum Hicoreae sprouted across loosely connected landscapes that would eventually cleave into North America, Asia, and Europe. Sixteen million years later the genus *Carya*, which encompasses all hickories (including the pecan), came into being. This genus died out in Europe by the Pleistocene period (2 million years ago) but took deep root in limited geographical ranges across Asia and North America. The pecan has become, according to one authority, "the largest, fastest-growing, best-known, most valuable, and one of the longest-lived of all the hickories."[4]

It was in North America alone, however, that the pecan found a climate amicable enough to inspire permanence. Wet, loamy, alluvial soil that reached from northern Illinois (hence its scientific name) to the Gulf Coast, and from central Texas to (possibly) a small patch of central Alabama, nurtured the pecan's exclusive development in North America. As the Stuart Pecan Company would brag in 1893, "We [Americans] have rightfully a monopoly upon the nut." This was exactly the case. The pecan thrives especially well along the turgid Mississippi and its arterial network of toffee-colored tributaries. As a botanical specimen, the pecan tree is supremely hardy—"a seasoned, professional athlete in a room of earnest but average sportsmen," as one team of botanists put it. It evolved a remarkable set of adaptive qualities that served it immensely well before the cooperative support of human cultivation. As a "climax tree species"—that is, as a species that does not care much for shade—the pecan successfully elbowed out potential competitors for the privilege of darting skyward and basking in direct sunlight. "The Pecan," declares a modern guide to American trees, "is intolerant of competition."[5]

The tree's robust root system is equally aggressive. It plunges to the water table and fans out far enough horizontally to absorb a consistent supply of surface moisture. These roots develop well before the tree shoots upward. "It is nothing unusual," wrote the famous plant breeder Luther Burbank, "to find pecan seedlings an inch high with roots from four to six feet in length." In this sense, its strength remains hidden from view. Nutrient uptake in the pecan root network happens most efficiently at the humus-surface layer, a critical sliver of soil where nutrients are especially dense. The pecan's evolution in regions that experience both the occasional ice storm and static heat waves has led the tree to select genes for modest drought and freeze tolerance. All things considered, the pecan possesses an enviable set of genetic and physical attributes. Significantly, these attributes work best in a narrow locality—namely, but not exclusively, the American South. It is the state tree of not only Texas but Mississippi and Arkansas as well.[6]

The pecan tree's promiscuity has helped its cause immeasurably. Wild pecans are social. They cluster densely in groves and pollinate from tree to tree, rather than within a single specimen. This happens because an individual tree's male and female flowers tend to bloom weeks apart. It lacks, according to one geographer, "self-pollinating mechanisms." This mismatch enhances the genetic diversity that provides the basis for the tree's dominant presence throughout riverine forests. No modern plant geneticist equipped with the most sophisticated tools could have designed a better complement to the tree's native, if relatively confined, habitat. Much of this adaptability, oddly enough, has to do with the tree's inability to mate with itself.[7]

If the native pecan covers a continuous swath from Mexico to Illinois, the densest pecan groves took shape in the alluvial ridges (just beyond the normal flood range) along the rich tributaries of Oklahoma, Texas, and Louisiana. It was here that they were able to best compete for light and space in pre-cisely the right soil among other native plants—a competition that made the wild pecan one of the tallest indigenous trees west of the Mississippi River, sometimes growing to 180 feet. It was also here that the soil drained but remained moist—a finicky prerequisite for extensive pecan roots. River bottom locations experienced less-dramatic temperature fluctuations, another favorable quality for pecan growth. Once the trees took root, a number of animal species that thrived along rivers began to consume and disperse seeds in all directions. Such species included wood ducks, wild turkeys, quail, crows, foxes, and squirrels. As these animals chose nuts that were easier to crack into, they became the first passive breeders, selecting for thinner-shelled pecans.[8]

For all these reasons, pecan trees were thriving in southern North America when Native Americans crossed the Bering Strait, or perhaps entered by boat farther down the Pacific coast, from Asia into North America. These intrepid no-mads—America's first immigrants—spanned the hemisphere in search of woolly beasts, eventually fracturing into thou-sands of distinct cultures of hunter-gatherers. In time, several groups reached the Mississippi River Valley, where they created cultures under grove after grove of towering pecan trees—trees that should have been nowhere else but exactly where they were. Understanding precisely how Native Americans worked the pecan tree into their myriad cultural expressions constitutes the first episode in the larger story of human-ity's ongoing relationship with America's most economically significant indigenous tree.[9]

CHAPTER I

The Native Americans' Nut

The beasts that lured the Native Americans to North America eventually died out. This was the result of a warming trend that start- ed about 16,000 years ago. Indians responded by forming more-stable, semi-nomadic cultures. Momentous agricultural changes ensued, and with the receding of the Tioga glaciers, Indians of the Lower Mississippi region started to pay seri- ous attention to readily available plant food, including the pecan. They began their relationship with the pecan tree by haphazardly harvesting pecans as part of their periodic hunting-gathering ventures. As pecans became increasingly popular, Indians intensified the harvest by swatting canopies with tall sticks and reaping showers of rewards—a technique that Anglo planters later adopted and carried well into the twentieth century. Although Indians would never establish pecan orchards per se—as they did with small plots of corn, beans, and squash—some evidence suggests that they pur- posefully spread pecan seeds to extend the range of what was becoming an essential ingredient in their evolving diet. In this respect, Native Americans were the tree's first human domesticators. (Although they would have had nothing on nonhuman fauna that had been spreading the pecan for more than 28 million years!)[1]

The word "pecan" derives from an Algonquin word meaning, loosely translated, "a nut too hard to crack by hand." Once gathered, the nut was indeed difficult to extract—but not *that* difficult. The reward, in essence, was worth the labor. What really mattered to the Indians was the fact that native pecans had comparatively thin shells—thanks, as we have seen, to the squirrels and crows that harvested them. Pecan meat was not going to fall from its casing without effort, but in a preindustrial age, it was more than readily accessible to anyone who had a rock and a hard, flat surface. The Mississippian cultures naturally embraced the pecan as enthusiastically as they did any other food source that qualified as low-hanging fruit. The Indian diet was already impressively diverse, consisting of more than 1,100 species of plants. The pecan became one of the most important, and in hundreds of cultures it was incorporated as a staple food. A further benefit, of course, was that pecan meat wasn't bitter. The wild pecan has, most agree, a delicious buttery flavor.[2]

The pecan served the Indians well. It is with some justice (and not a little irony) that today's most popular cultivars are named after Native American peoples: Pawnee, Cheyenne, Kiowa, Mohawk, Choctaw, and Wichita, to name only a few. The pecan is a supremely healthy nut. A hundred grams of wild pecans (about two handfuls) pack a nutritional punch: 718 calories, 9.7 grams of protein, 2.4 grams of fiber, 74 grams of fat, and significant doses of critical micronutrients such as iron, potassium, magnesium, beta-carotene, thiamine, riboflavin, niacin, and ascorbic acid. Pecans help maintain healthy lipid levels while providing a powerful array of antioxidants. These healthful qualities were critical for calorically (and sometimes nutritionally) challenged hunter-gatherers. Consider the linolenic and stearic acids in the pecan, as well as its monosaturated oil, and it's no wonder that the Indians shook the trees every fall, gathering up superfood along the region's extensive riverbanks. As Indians were quick to discern, this was cheap, healthy sustenance obtained with scant expenditure of labor.[3]

In the pre-Columbian era, the pecan tree came to fit seamlessly into evolving Native American foraging strategies. Pecan nuts quickly became a tasty food that Indians living from Texas to Arkansas to Louisiana eagerly consumed alongside their cultivated beans, corn, melons, and squash. The nuts nicely complemented their broader menu of foraged items, including crab apples, persimmons, sassafras, wild millet, pond lilies, huckleberries, plums, and papaws. Occasional doses of bear, possum, deer, and swamp rabbit rounded out the constantly shifting, inherently flexible Native American menu. Indians primarily ate pecans whole—in many ways this was the food's greatest allure. They also pounded them into a powder, applied the pecan dust to corn gruel and bread, worked pecan meal into bison meat, and even boiled nuts to ease the extraction of meat. Others may have fermented pecan powder into an alcoholic beverage called *powcohicora*. Perhaps not incidentally, there's currently a brewery in Mississippi that uses pecan meal in lieu of hops.[4]

Pecans influenced more than the Native American diet. The Indians' decision to consume pecan nuts as a steady component of their overall diet had a direct influence on Native American mobility as well. One thing about the pecan tree that made it especially influential—if quirky—was that it does not produce nuts every year.[5] If you have a pecan tree in your yard, you have likely noticed that it is "alternate bearing." This is certainly the case with the pecan tree that rockets through my back deck in Austin. The nuts fall in abundance every two to four years. It is hard to say why pecans exhibit this trait. Early botanists once thought alternate masting meant that the tree was tired and needed rest. This is probably wrong. Nonetheless, it should be said that, even today, as the extension agency at Louisiana State University puts it, "the exact cause of alternate bearing continues to elude researchers."

One interesting hypothesis is that pecans mast inconsistently as a strategy designed to outsmart insects. By denying mast to voracious pecan weevils on a reliable schedule (to cite just one pest that attacks the pecan), the tree is able to reduce insect populations during "off" years before shifting into high gear and producing nuts when the insect populations are down and unable to recover fast enough to exact real damage. It could also be that the carbohydrates needed to build a nut as dense and nutritious as the pecan simply take more time to develop. Photosynthesis, in essence, might very well need more time to engineer seeds with an oil content as high as 74 percent. Whatever the reason, this botanical oddity not only influenced those who depended on it as integral to their sustenance, but defines the pecan tree, even the cultivated varieties, to this day.[6]

In any case, it seems that inconsistent masting partially influenced the course of Indians' nomadic movements. One grove would mast one year, while another grove, situated in a distant river flat in another region, would mast the next. Indians must have thought this to be odd. Deer would travel the same general route every season. Corn, beans, and squash would annually cluster over each other in the same beds. Fish would return to spawn in the same soft eddies. Berries would fatten on the same vines and bushes as they always had done. Pecans, however, defied the seasonal cycles of predictable abundance and scarcity, masting in a less reliable and uniform manner, following vague patterns rather than precise schedules. For a people deeply attuned to seasonal predictability, this aspect of the pecan tree must have been at least a little disorienting.[7]

Fortunately, when masting was abundant it was conspicuously so. It is thus no surprise that the archaeological evidence suggests that Indians adjusted their lives to the pecan's odd timing, enjoying its meat enough to adapt their perennial migrations—however casual they may have been—to these haphazard masting schedules. Piecing together any sort of exact map of movement is impossible. There's evidence, however, of south Texas Indians traveling up to 120 kilometers to reap the offerings of especially productive groves. The pecan trees, to an extent, told them where to go. Indians, fully sold on the nut's worth, followed. Many groups of Indians—including the Comanche, Caddo, and Kickapoo—may even have settled where they did as a direct result of proximity to a variety of well-known and highly productive pecan groves.[8]

In time, a nascent pecan trade developed among the Indians. When the Mescalero Apaches drove bison herds from Colorado to the Concho River in Texas each winter, they were reliably met by Mississippians hauling baskets of pecans for exchange. The Anaqua Indians, who lived in coastal Texas, traveled to the Colorado River every winter, where they set up camp for about six months. On their journey, the Anaqua gathered pecans and traded them with other Indian cultures as they traveled. From New Mexico came Mescalero Indians, who established winter camps along the San Saba, Pedernales, and Llano Rivers. Settling temporarily in these pecan-abundant regions, the Mescalero hauled pecans back to New Mexico, trading them with Indians scattered throughout west Texas. The Jumano Indians maintained thriving villages in both the Jumano Mountains of New Mexico and the Rio Grande Valley, with satellite settlements in the upper Colorado and Concho Valleys. The Jumanos were thus constantly crisscrossing the region, distributing pecans from pecan-rich to pecan-poor areas, sharing the natural wealth.[9]

This trade easily and profitably segued into exchange with non-Indian groups. When Spaniards arrived in the sixteenth century, they encountered Indians hawking pecans from the upper Colorado River to the lower Rio Grande Valley. Diverse native cultures crossed paths repeatedly in the extended and worked-over flats of rivers and streams, and the means of exchange during these interactions typically involved pecans.

In the 1680s, one Jumano Indian told a Spaniard about "Las Nueces"—a river where "there are nuts in such abundance . . . that they constitute the maintenance of many nations who enjoy friendship and barter and exchange" together. Trying to redeem souls in the Caddo region of east Texas, Fray Isidoro de Espinosa watched Indians "gather quantities of thick shelled nuts to last a whole year." The Caddos strung the nut meats on long cords and stored them in leather sacs to draw upon throughout the winter and spring as edible snacks and valued commodities for trade. The pecan was, in a sense, both legal tender and lingua franca.[10]

Although the Indians never created anything even remotely resembling commercial orchards, there is every reason to believe that they roughly cultivated pecans to foster this indigenous but increasingly active commerce throughout the weblike riverine network of the Mississippi River Valley. None of these efforts should distract us from the fact that when it came to pecans, pre-contact Indians along the Mississippi and its tributaries were essentially opportunistic gatherers, always overshadowed in their cultivation efforts by squirrels and crows. Even if Indians weren't active cultivators of pecans, though, the nuts nonetheless encouraged them to harvest in a timely and efficient manner. When it comes to pre-contact cultures, we generally lack details about how Indians might have precisely streamlined harvesting methods to improve the efficacy of collection. They left us few scraps of evidence, none of them written. We can be fairly certain, though, that the pressure to harvest with alacrity was high, and that Indians responded with a timeliness and ingenuity characteristic of their overall approach to harvesting food.

Among the motivating factors for harvesting with diligence were numerous species from across the animal kingdom. A prominent motivation to gather nuts at the opportune time would have been the abundant squirrel population (as well as other small mammals). When pecans ripen they release an odor. This smell would have wafted across the forest floor and into squirrel dens, triggering squirrels to forage for what was essentially the region's densest natural food. Anyone who has observed squirrels at work knows that they can, with remarkable self-possession, clear a dense spread of fallen nuts with vacuum-like dedication. There's a reason why they're called the "pecan tree's feet." Without competition from humans, a few dozen gray squirrels living within a kilometer of a single pecan tree can consume or bury every nut the tree produces (two hundred to six hundred) in a matter of six weeks. It was therefore critically important that Indians arrive either just before or immediately after the pecans began to mast. If they lagged, squirrels were sure to make a significant dent in the pecan supply. (As one Texas pecan grower explains on his website: "Eat Pecans! 10,000,000 squirrels can't be wrong.")[11]

Some firsthand accounts bearing on squirrels and pecans suggest that squirrels would even have denuded pecan trees while the nuts were still on the tree, still encased in their four-valved green husks, thereby effectively outdoing the Indians. This hypothesis, however, is a dubious one. A recollection by Roy Bedichek, the great Texas naturalist, goes some way toward casting doubt on the claim. Observing the "ravages" of the rock squirrel upon a pecan forest, he wrote, "Impatient for this favorite food, he gnaws the green outer covering down to the shell of the nut itself, where the bitter juice bites his thievish tongue, and then throws the nut down." Over the course of five minutes, Bedichek watched forty-six nuts hit the ground as a result of this capricious sampling. One could argue that not only were squirrels a poor competitor for pecans in the tree, but they actually made it easier for the Indians—if they arrived at the right moment—to obtain the partially husked nuts. By littering them across the forest floor, the squirrels reduced the time Indians had to spend beating the tree with large sticks and searching the crowded forest floor for dividends.[12]

Another wild animal Indians had to watch was the crow. These keenly intelligent, tool-wielding birds either pluck pecan nuts from the branches or harvest them from the ground. Their method of cracking the shell is worth noting. According to an early-twentieth-century zoologist (who far outdid Bedichek by spending months observing a single flock of American crows cavort about a pecan orchard): "They [the crows] would alight on posts, hold the pecans with their feet and peck at them until the shells split, or until they pecked a hole through them." When a hole was bored, "they inserted the bill and beat the pecan against the post." This diligent scientist went on to observe that this process worked best for longer nuts, a fact that the crows were evidently able to appreciate and, in no time, exploit. (When pavement came about, crows quickly learned to fly up and drop the nuts upon it, too. As noted, the "black denizen of forest and field" is not a stupid bird.)[13]

Crows were thus not to be ignored. All Indians could hope for when it came to crows was that the birds found other foods to eat when they encountered pecan groves. They will, ornithologists commonly observe, eat a wide array of foods (stomach dissections of crows have yielded more than 650 different kinds of plant and animal products). But as with the pecan, we shouldn't rush to the conclusion that competitors didn't deliver unintended advantages. The crows were also of help to the Indians. Their ceaselessly grating cackles may have intensified when it was time for pecans to be harvested. Native Americans, attuned as they could be to the subtlest of nature's intonations, tended to act upon such announcements.

While squirrels and crows may have been immediate competitors with Indians for a local stash of wild pecans, in the long term their presence proved to be exceptionally beneficial to pecan proliferation. These animals, as it turns out, were ultimately critical in extending the pecan tree's range, certainly much more than any two-legged creature could systematically accomplish. The pecan nut closely co-evolved with these animals over many millions of years. A larger nut was more attractive to animals that were able to move it from one location to another. As a reward for their services, mammals would eat some nuts but not all of them. Squirrels in particular would often bury nuts far and wide, rarely making it back to retrieve the entirety of what they planted. Crows would carry nuts and frequently drop them in new locations, from which point the squirrels would scurry over and bury them. These relatively hidden but seminal events were undoubtedly good news for the longevity of the pecan tree.

The perpetual dance between animal and plant is often called mutualism. Before the emergence of this mutualism, eras and eras ago, the pecan tree needed the wind to move its "winged nutlets" from one region to another. Pecan trees, in other words, did not always have big, edible seeds. As squirrels became squirrels, and crows became crows, winged nutlets became wingless nuts. The mutualism that co-evolved remains evident to anyone who, like Bedichek or Gilbert White, spends quality time observing the many melodramas that unfold under a tree. Not to get too far ahead of the story, but when one observes how commercial pecan orchards work today, it becomes perfectly clear that the farmer's goal, when you get right down to it, is to exchange mutualism for botanical dominance. In a sense, the Indians established the starting point from which this ambitious and potentially devastating process of domination would proceed. Before humans, though, it was all about the wind, birds, squirrels, and, of course, the vagaries of evolutionary change.[14]

When it came to pecan access, Indians also benefited from ecological factors beyond their control, much less recognition—factors that we can appreciate only from the perch of the present. A potential predator of pecan nuts—one that (as we will later see) would threaten to devastate cultivated pecan orchards throughout the Southeast and Southwest—was the pecan weevil. The Indians, however, had no need to fear the pecan weevil because it and other potential insect predators were effectively controlled by the red-headed woodpecker, which at the time thrived in numbers high enough to keep the weevil in balance. "The redhead," one ornithologist wrote in the 1920s, "is very fond of insects." And so it was throughout pecan territory. By the nineteenth century, though, with the systematic harvesting of snags (fallen timber), red-headed woodpeckers (which relied on the snags as a primary food source) diminished in number, providing a small but critical berth for the weevil. As is true of most invasive insects, the weevil did not need much of a chance to proliferate to invasive proportions. But for pre-contact Indians, natural control kept the weevil, and other like-minded insect predators, in balance.[15]

Another pecan predator that had yet to arrive in significant numbers was the raccoon. Today, raccoons pursue urban and suburban garbage as their primary source of food. This, however, is a relatively recent dietary change. Writing about raccoons in southern Illinois in the 1940s, one wildlife biologist noted, "Pecan nuts undoubtedly contribute much to the excellent condition of raccoons," suggesting that raccoons had always been a fierce competitor for pecans. In pre-contact North America, however, that was not the case. Raccoons would not have been prevalent (if existent at all) in regions where the pecan grew. The reason is that the expansion of European-style agriculture, plus later urbanization, was the primary factor that eventually drove the raccoon out of the far southeastern corner of the United States and into trash cans across the Northern Hemisphere. In pre-contact days, though, raccoons would have known no pecans, for the simple reason that they did not share space with native pecan groves.[16]

One shouldn't overlook the wood rat as a pecan predator. This rodent, which would become an especially vigorous competitor for pecans in the Brazos Valley, was also not yet a factor for the Indians. Its numbers were similarly monitored by natural control, specifically the abundance of hawks, owls, and rat snakes that prevailed before aggressive deforestation and agricultural development. Its decline, which seems to have begun in the late nineteenth century, led to a situation in which, according to one early-twentieth-century wild-life biologist, "native rats and mice have so increased their numbers that their depredations have assumed almost the proportions of a plague." Again, this is a relatively recent development, one that would not have impinged upon Indian access to their native nuts. Rats, raccoons, weevils—plus dozens of other species—would go on to compete for pecans in groves throughout North America. When Native Americans were eating pecans before European arrival, however, these animals were too involved in other ecological relationships to bother much with pecans.[17]

Once acquired by Indians, pecans enjoyed a couple of key advantages over other foraged foods. For one thing, they did not have to be consumed in their entirety all at once. This was not the case for animal meat, which was perishable (unless it was jerked or smoked—both quite labor-intensive tasks and, as a result, infrequently undertaken). There are many accounts of Indians fresh off an extended hunt gorging themselves on weeks' worth of animal flesh before it perished. Nuts, which had the additional benefit of requiring minimal processing, could be harvested and stored for months, if not years. Indians did not have to gorge on pecans for the sole purpose of not wasting them.

Storage, however, was considered serious business. Nuts had to be secreted in places where rodents and mammals could not penetrate—as they were much better at raiding human stash than humans were at raiding animal stash. Many cultures relied on capacious earthen pits, rock shelters, and caves. Archaeologists have unearthed human-secreted pecan remains dating as far back as 6700 BC. Evidence has been scraped out of Baker Cave in Texas, the Cope Site in Louisiana, and Modoc Rock Shelter in Illinois. Pecans stored well, and Indians would usually take up to two months to deplete their reserves. They could have taken longer had they so wished. The pecan can be kept in a dry, cool place (at about 47 degrees Fahrenheit) for as long as a year without drying out. Some have speculated that Indians may have stored nuts in the hollowed-out trunks of pecan trees, noting that squirrels keep upwards of 45 kilograms of nuts in such natural cubbies.[18]

Nuts had the further advantage of having a superb energy cost/benefit ratio. In a land-rich but labor-poor environment, this asset may have been the greatest as far as the Indians were concerned. Modern estimates suggest that it would have been possible for a single Indian to harvest 6.2 kilograms of nuts per hour. Armed with hammer stones and a properly chosen rock surface, it takes an individual about an hour to extract 66 grams of meat, a volume that amounts to about 450 kilocalories of food energy. Scaling up these figures places matters in eye-opening perspective. According to one estimate, the average harvest of native pecans from Texas, Oklahoma, and Louisiana would have been 10,138,336 kilograms of nut meat per annual masting. This amount of calories, if harvested, would have been equivalent in weight to the meat of 17,000 to 25,600 bison! Evaluating these numbers, Texas botanist Grant Hall writes, "Where a bison with a body weight of 476 kg was shown to have edible parts with a food energy value of 453,000 kcal, an average native pecan native nut harvest would be equivalent in food value to upwards of 150,000 bison."[19]

As is so often the case when we try to probe cultures that left no written record, we tend to be left with more questions than answers. Did pre-contact Indians turn pecan harvests into social events? Did they pioneer any especially ingenious methods of dealing with crows and squirrels? Did they develop ceremonies or rituals that involved pecans? Did they enjoy the taste of these buttery nuts or was it all about energy? Did they have special pecan recipes? Elusive questions, all of them. What we do know, however, is important, and worth reiterating. We know that Indians developed an early form of human mutualism with pecan trees. They had no need to harvest pecan wood, so pecan trees were never systematically removed from the landscape—as were, say, pines for hunting and firewood, and the osage orange for bow making. Because Indians found the pecan's seeds to be the most valuable aspect of the tree, and the densest plant food around, they formed their diets, migratory patterns, and trading networks around the tree's bounty, haphazard as the masting may have been. In so doing, they helped pecans proliferate as they increasingly enjoyed a food source that was rich in nutrients, relatively easy to access, and seamlessly adaptable to the changing natural environment of the American South.

If the pre-contact period remains a relative black hole of information, one small but telling request, made hundreds of years after contact, leaves us with some concrete sense of the pecan's lasting place in Native American material and cultural life. The request came from the tribal government of the Chickasaw Nation, which included in its new constitution a choice stipulation, one of only a handful of requests, and thus one that surely meant a lot to them as a culture precariously clinging to its identity. It demanded "an act against the destroying of pecan trees." As we will see, this request, even after European contact, was, however improbably, honored in the breach by white men whose relationship with the environment turned out to follow radically different rules.[20]

CHAPTER 2

"Pekan Nuttrees"

EUROPEANS ENCOUNTER THE PECAN

When Christopher Columbus arrived in the New World, he initiated the most comprehensive exchange of food and drink the world had ever experienced. Corn, tomatoes, and potatoes went east. Wheat, olives, and livestock went west. Pretty much anything edible and shippable was packed into hogsheads or loaded into pens and sent crisscrossing the Atlantic. So many plants and animals found a comfortable home in foreign soil that the global landscape was fundamentally (and permanently) altered within a century after discovery. The list is virtually endless. European grasses and clovers carpeted the pastures of North America. American grapevines snaked up European trellises. Peruvian potatoes rooted in Irish soil. South American tomatoes brightened Italian gardens. Indian corn filled English feed troughs. French peaches grew in North American orchards. Onions, garlic, parsley, coriander, and oregano altered the New World diet and landscape as much as beans, chile peppers, squash, and agave did the Old World's. This cross-fertilization truly changed the global diet.[1]

Pecans, however, generally stayed out of the Columbian exchange. Although they were by far the most significant native American nut growing in the New World, and although the Spaniards brought barrels of pecan samples back to the

Old World, Europeans never embraced pecans with the kind of enthusiasm we might expect. They did not transform and co-opt them the way they did so many other crops indigenous to the New World (say, the potato, the tomato, corn). The decision not to cultivate pecans with any real fervor in the Old World continues to this day. Pecan trees—all cultivated varieties—can be found sparsely in Israel, South Africa, and Australia. Nevertheless, according to *The Oxford Companion to Food*, they are "still little known outside N. America and Mexico."[2]

This point matters more than it might seem. When we contemplate the history of the pecan tree, we're contemplating the history of a plant that not only is native to North America but also has the rare distinction of remaining largely confined to the region where it originated. It's a botanical homebody in an age of floral wanderlust. To this day, virtually all pecans produced for commercial purposes are grown in the southern portion of the United States (mainly Texas, New Mexico, and Georgia). Throughout most of human history, the vast majority of pecans have been consumed at home. Pecans, in essence, are native nuts that have largely remained on native turf. This is unusual.[3]

To begin understanding exactly why this is the case, it is necessary to make a brief detour down a related path of natural history, one that leads to another nut that shares many of the pecan's culinary qualities: the walnut. The walnut tree is in the same family as the pecan—Juglandaceae. Whereas the pecan colonized an expanse of southern North America, however, the European walnut colonized a much wider swath of the global landscape—territories extending all the way from southeastern Europe to Asia. Much like pecans, walnuts have been gathered, stored, cracked, roasted, and eaten whole since thousands of years before the dawn of agriculture. Also like pecans, they're an ideal forage crop. Unlike pecans, though, the walnut had a much larger native geographical range, several more immediate uses, and exposure to groups of global travelers seemingly interested in planting it everywhere they set foot.

The Persians pressed walnut oil and sold it throughout the Mediterranean, especially to the ancient Greeks. The French valued walnut wood for furniture making, as did the English after the importation of the walnut across the channel in the fifteenth century. The Chinese used walnuts to make ketchup. Other cultures pickled them and ate them as a condiment throughout the year. Romans enjoyed the nuts so much that they tossed them at newlyweds during wedding celebrations. Walnut leaves were commonly employed by many cultures as a swift and thorough laxative.[4] Everyone throughout Europe and Asia seemed to appreciate the taste, use, and high productivity of walnuts (they are not alternate bearing). The walnut has consistently been a remarkably popular and versatile nut—and that is precisely why the walnut matters for the pecan. It was so popular and versatile that it would have been redundant to have imported and cultivated a nut so similar to it as the pecan. It would have been a waste of energy. In essence, where the walnut existed, and where the walnut traveled and took root, the pecan had little reason to go.[5]

It could thus be said that the walnut played a deterrent role in the pecan's geographical expansion. This was the case not only in Europe but in North America as well. The European walnut was so enthusiastically cultivated by Europeans that when they came to the New World, settlers felt they could not do without it—its superior wood, sweet meat, and curative leaves were too valuable to forgo in an unfamiliar landscape. The tree was thus eventually planted in those very regions of North America where native pecan groves did not reach. In the east, it joined and eventually overtook the native black walnut in New England. Writing in 1847, the American botanist Andrew Jackson Downing called the European walnut "a fine lofty growing tree, with a handsome spreading head, and bearing large and excellent nuts." It was a tree that he was sure would be "profitable . . . for the market." Spanish missionaries planted the European walnut throughout California in the 1800s with equally prolific consequences. Today, 75 percent of the commercial walnut production in the world occurs in the central valley of California.[6]

In essence, whenever and wherever Europeans arrived in the New World, they brought with them European walnuts to plant. The European walnut, in turn, helped hem the pecan in in its native habitat. So inconsequential did the pecan seem beyond its indigenous border that when Downing wrote his comprehensive book on American fruit trees in the mid–nineteenth century, the pecan did not even get a mention. As late as 1915, the famous plant breeder Luther Burbank was openly wishing for hardier pecan cultivars "so that the pecan might be cultivated further to the north." The interest in taking the pecan north, however, never materialized. The fact that no northern cultivars existed by that date is a telling testament to the walnut's incredible promiscuity and the pecan's contrasting provincialism. It also helps explain why the pecan stayed in place.[7]

The pecan tree's tendency to stay near home had a lot to do with precisely why the pecan was valued as it was. Pecan wood was little needed as a building material, much less as fuel. Writing in 1908, the civil engineer Charles Henry Snow explained how "the pecan affords wood so inferior as to be little used in construction." The major problem with pecan wood is that without the use of industrial blowers, it is extremely difficult to dry. Even in the modern era it requires, according to one specialist in wood quality, "7–15 days in the kiln to dry 1-inch lumber from green to 6 percent moisture." An 1874 newspaper article on wood types called the pecan "a wood not so valuable by any means." In preindustrial times it would have been far too heavy, as a result of its moisture content, to haul over long distances. Today, pecan wood is dried through intensive industrial methods and is used for furniture making, flooring (mainly for gymnasiums), cabinetry, and architectural trim—all of which would have been largely irrelevant to both the Indians and the Europeans who first encountered the dense groves of pecan trees. This reputation of being less than an ideal building material continues to this day. As the U.S. Department of Agriculture (USDA) Forest Service currently explains, "Pecan wood is inferior to that of other hickories and is not important commercially."[8]

Awareness of the walnut's benefits, in addition to the pecan's inferiority as a building material or a reliable source of fuel, thereby managed to keep it exclusively rooted in its natively circumscribed zone. Even more important than these factors, though, was the fact that the pecan was valued for one characteristic above all others: the quality of its nuts. So when Europeans—namely, the Spanish and the French— finally encountered the pecan, they did so not on their own turf and on their own terms, as they did with so many other plants and animals brought back to Europe. Instead, Europeans witnessed the pecan as travelers and explorers dealing with a radically new landscape, one inhabited by strange new cultures and bearing bizarre, oblong, bronzed new fruit. Fruit that, as we will find, they often saw as, alas, a type of walnut.

Isolation was an unusual situation for a fruit–bearing tree to be in during the era after Columbus's discovery. The movement of biomass eastward across the Atlantic became so intense that most Europeans first saw common New World plants in a European garden or marketplace. Once European adventurers exhausted efforts to discover gold and silver deposits in the resource-rich Americas, they turned to botanical exploration. Very often exploration turned to exploitation, and exploitation to biopiracy, as Europeans sought profit from the potential riches sprouting out of the soil rather than continuing to seek the ores beneath it. Just to see the pecan, much less eat it, Europeans were going to have to travel. Indeed, unless one had a friend with eccentric botanical interests or an experimental garden, the pecan would have to be witnessed on the rugged and hotly contested terrain of southern North America.[9]

When they initially came across the native nut, Spanish and French travelers more often than not judged it to be a walnut. As Cabeza de Vaca traveled from Galveston to the Guadalupe River in 1533, he recalled approaching "the place of which we had been told to eat walnuts." De Vaca's walnuts were pecans. He added that these mysterious dense nuts were "ground with a small kind of grain and this is the subsistence of the people two months in the year without any other thing." Whatever he thought he was seeing, de Vaca was so impressed with their swollen abundance that he described the Guadalupe as "a river of nuts." Lope de Oviedo, a member of de Vaca's exploration party, stressed the importance of these sweet oval nuggets, mentioning how "there were on the banks of the river many nuts, which the Indians ate in their season, coming from twenty or thirty leagues round about." He too thought he was looking at a walnut, but noted that "these nuts were much smaller than those [walnuts] of Spain."[10] Hernando de Soto, the first European to cross the Mississippi River, offered more of the same assessment. He referred to "much oil of walnuts which is clear and of good taste" when, in actuality, he was almost certainly appreciating the benefits of pecan oil.[11] When the French voyager Penicault first saw the pecan while traveling in the Natchez region in 1704, he described it as "similar enough to the walnuts of Europe." His fellow Frenchman Antoine-Simon Le Page du Pratz observed that the Mississippi River was lined with trees bearing "a very small kind of walnut . . . more delicate than our own, less oily." Even as late as the 1770s, the Spanish traveler Antonio de Ulloa described "Pecanos" as, yet again, a "kind of walnut." It is commonly noted that colonial explorers and adventurers tended to interpret New World phenomena in Old World terms. This was certainly true with the Spanish and French reaction to the foreign pecan.[12]

Such cultural expressions were predictable enough. A handful of travelers, though, were quicker to bear witness to the pecan as something altogether new to their experience. The Frenchman André Malraux described the nut in its own terms—or, more to the point, in terms that Indians were using. In 1795 he found a grove of pecans in southern Illinois and called the fruits "Pekan Nuttrees." By the late seventeenth century most Spanish travelers were mentioning pecan trees as an iconic aspect of the southern landscape. When, in 1693, Gregorio de Salinas Varona traveled from the San Marcos region of central Texas to what is now Palestine, Texas (in order to resupply a team of Spanish missionaries), he recorded in his journal being impressed by "a grove of pecan trees" as he and his party crossed the Nueces River— which, appropriately, was named by Alonso de León for the abundant pecans lining it. Several days later Varona awoke and "departed at six o'clock in the morning through a grove of oak and pecan trees." A few days afterward, riding "in a northeasterly direction through a very sandy plain," he wove his way through stands of "oaks, live oaks, and pecan trees." These references to pecan trees might seem to be perfunctory lines in an explorer's journal. To the contrary, the fact that Europeans were singling them out for mention suggests that they were perceived as nothing less than an outstanding aspect of an already strange and unfamiliar landscape.[13]

French voyagers, most of whom made their way through pecan country in the early eighteenth century, not only generally knew the pecan to be a pecan, but they were highly complimentary of the tree's qualities. P. F. Charlevoix, traveling through "Kaskaquias" (somewhere in southern Illinois) in 1721, confided to his journal how "among the fruits that are peculiar to this country the most remarkable are the pecans." He described the nut as having "the length and form of a large acorn" and admired its "fine and delicate taste." Charlevoix's countryman, the priest Pierre-Gabriel Marest, rated the "nuttree" as having "a better flavor than our nuts in France," a certain reference to the walnut. In 1758, Le Page du Prazt extolled the pecans as having "a flavor so fine that the French make 'pralines' of them as good as those made of almonds." This New World version of an old French confection would, as we will later see, go on to become a staple of New Orleans' culinary heritage.[14]

The English, who were cautious latecomers to the game of colonization, were cautious latecomers to the native nut as well. They never ventured far enough into the North American interior before the French and Indian War (1754–1763) to discover pecan trees in their indigenous environment. It is most likely the case that pecans never traveled to the Atlantic seaboard before 1760, when fur traders finally began transporting pecan nuts from the Mississippi Valley to New York (if for no other reason than to show them off as exotic curiosities from the frontier). Colonial British America's notably eccentric and impassioned naturalist John Bartram was the most eager of any colonial American to introduce the pecan into the English botanical establishment. Bartram laid out his plans in 1761 in a letter to his London counterpart, Peter Collinson. "I have not been to Ohio," he wrote. "But in two weeks I hope to set out to search myself if the barbarous Indians don't hinder me (and if I die a martyr to botany, God's will be done)."[15]

His exploratory plan was simple enough. With the Ohio River Valley finally open to unimpeded British exploration and settlement (the French had been decisively routed at the Battle of Quebec in 1760), Bartram would hike west in search of floral novelties and send his most prized discoveries back to his friend, mentor, and devout Quaker Collinson. This he did as scheduled. However, when Collinson unwrapped the pecans that Bartram had gathered during his "ramblings on the Ohio," he delivered the first recorded English review of the pecan. He panned it. "I really believe my honest John is a great wag," he explained, "and has sent me seven hard, stony seeds, something shaped like an acorn, to puzzle us."[16] As it turned out, Collinson's remark more or less summed up what would be the reaction of British Americans to the pecan. It was indeed a puzzling nut to the British colonists—odd-looking, not exactly a walnut, and, as they quickly realized, stubbornly difficult to propagate in the eastern portion of North America and, even more so, in English soil. Bartram's eventual response to Collinson hardly pushed Collinson's opinion in a more enthusiastic direction. He dutifully praised the kernel for being "very sweet" but added of the nuts he had sent: "I am afraid they won't sprout."[17]

Bartram's dud samples notwithstanding, a trickle of pecans continued to flow to the east coast from the Ohio River Valley, traveling in the worn pockets of wayward traders, land developers, and tireless surveyors. By 1772 William Prince, colonial America's first commercial nurseryman, planted thirty pecan nuts at his fruit orchard in Flushing, Long Island. Ten saplings sprouted, eight of which Prince packed tightly in sand and shipped to England, where they sold for ten guineas apiece. Two he left rooted in Long Island soil for the purposes of someday gathering nuts for the occasional snack. Bartram himself planted a few pecans in his Philadelphia garden—how many we do not know, but we do know that at least one survived. A newspaper report from 1886 mentioned a pecan tree "on the Bartram estate . . . over 90 feet high." This was, however, more of a novelty than a trend, an exception that proved the rule of the pecan's absence on the eastern seaboard of North America.[18]

The rest of the pecan's history in British North America

is spotty. English botanist Humphry Marshall included the pecan in his 1773 book, *Arbustrum Americanum: The American Grove*, a quirky compendium of New World trees. Another planting of a pecan tree in British America happened in 1774, when William Hamilton, the keeper of a respected colonial garden outside of Philadelphia, planted an "Illinois hickory" (which the pecan was often called by the English). On March 25, 1775, George Washington planted, as he described them, "25 Mississippi Nuts—something like the pig nut—but longer, thinner shelld and fuller of meat." Given Washington's elevated status, March 25, according to Chase's Calendar of Events, is now officially "Pecan Day" in the United States. In 1781, Captain Wangenheim, a Hessian soldier employed by the British army in the Revolutionary War, published a thumbnail sketch of the pecan tree in a short book he wrote on American forests. In 1786 Washington sowed "21 of the Illinois nuts," using yet another moniker for the pecan. Two of those specimens survived into the twenty-first century, one of which had to be taken down in 2004 after being damaged by Hurricane Isabel. As for the fate of the aforementioned Long Island trees, we do not know when they fell. But we know that by 1799 Hamilton, the Philadelphia gardener, lamented the following effect of a heavy frost: "A tree, too, the only one I had of Juglans Pacane, or Illinois hickory, which I raised twenty-five years ago from seed, is entirely killed."[19]

If the pecan inspired only periodic bursts of enthusiasm on the east coast of colonial and early America, this general lack of interest could not be blamed on Thomas Jefferson, the man who succeeded Bartram as the tree's most enthusiastic advocate. Writing from Paris in January 1786, just as the young republic was languishing under the Articles of Confederation, he ended a lengthy letter to his friend Archibald Stuart with the following request: "I must add a prayer for some Paccan nuts, 100, if possible, to be packed in a box of sand and sent to me." We have no idea what happened to these nuts once they made it to France (or if they ever even made it to France, for that matter). What we do know is that Jefferson's curiosity about the pecan followed him back to America, where, on March 17, 1794, he recorded this accomplishment in his Garden Book: "Planted 200 paccan nuts." By 1802, while serving as president of the United States, he still found time to cultivate pecans. On May 26 he recorded how he "planted a great row of Paccan nuts, in the same rows as those planted in the last two years." In March 1812 he placed "25 paccans" into Monticello soil. Jefferson, who has been called "the father of American forestry," mostly stuck to landscaping Monticello with trees native to his "country," Virginia. However, the exotic pecan became one of his "pet trees," a specimen for which he maintained deep affection. None of the Monticello samples survive, but Jefferson's historical commitment to the tree remains admirably unimpeachable.[20]

Thomas Jefferson was as antimonarchist as any citizen on the planet. It thus comes as something of a surprise to hear that he once allegedly said, "I wish I was a despot." It was not people that Jefferson wanted to rule with an iron fist, but trees. "I wish I was a despot," he said, "that I might save the noble, beautiful trees that are daily falling sacrifice to the cupidity of their owners." Felling a tree unnecessarily, he added, "seems to me a crime little short of murder." Strong words from the Sage of Monticello. But Jefferson would have been pleased with the nineteenth-century fate of pecan trees, even if that fate would have to play out in a region far from the sacred soils of Virginia. Whereas the pecan never found a home along the east coast during the colonial and early American periods, it would go on to thrive as a passively cultivated "crop" throughout the American South. Perhaps more surprisingly, it would do so in a relatively wild state for most of the nineteenth and some of the twentieth centuries. Indeed, unlike any other fruit-bearing tree in the age of cultivation, the pecan managed to evade the cultivating hand of man for centuries after humans began exploiting it for food. Even in the early twentieth century, the "pecan industry" was nowhere near becoming a full-fledged commercial entity that treated trees as commodities. Rather, trees were still viewed as indigenous but generous members of a native habitat. It was the kind of habitat that Jefferson deeply valued, even as the events of a rapidly expanding nation were proving it to be a quaint relic of a bygone era.

"...the Forest into an Orchard"

Passive Cultivation on the Texas Frontier

Jefferson might have been pleased with the fate of the pecan, but his hopeful vision of forest preservation was otherwise dashed throughout the nineteenth century. Nowhere was the disregard more intense than in those very regions where native pecan groves traditionally thrived: the American South. A scene from William Faulkner's novella *The Bear* captures the specter of rampant deforestation as well as any work of historical scholarship. With quiet poignancy, protagonist Ike McCaslin observes Yoknapatawpha County's "new planing mill already half completed which would cover two or three acres." He notes its "light bright rust of newness and of piled crossties sharp with creosote." McCaslin elaborates on this scene, wistfully observing a logging train "vanish into the wilderness" like a "harmless snake vanishing into weeds."

It is a fine literary account. However, as far as native trees were concerned, this snake was far from harmless. The east coast had undergone massive deforestation back in the seventeenth and eighteenth centuries. Now, as McCaslin presciently forewarned, it was the South's turn to have its forests fall to the steady march of population and progress. In relatively short order, forests were transformed into fields, pioneers into industrialists. The American South excelled at these transformations as well as the North had ever done. However—and this is the critical point—the pecan escaped this nineteenth-century swath of destruction. Understanding the reasons for this escape and the implications of it is the goal of this chapter. Indeed, knowing how and why Texas pecan trees avoided the destructive environmental transformations that accompanied the nineteenth-century commercialization of Texas is an important part of explaining how Texas, by the end of the nineteenth century, had become, however temporarily, the world's epicenter of pecan production, harvesting, and exportation.[1]

Ike McCaslin mentioned only trains and mills. A perfect storm of other factors, however, converged to precipitate the demise of southern forests. Mainline carriers, extensive tramway systems, big-wheeled carts, commercial sawmills, virtually no environmental restrictions, and the concentrated ownership of lumber outfits all combined to establish the preconditions for the systematic removal of southeastern trees. This process came to bear especially hard on east Texas and Louisiana. By 1880 several prominent companies had constructed dozens of mill towns throughout these regions. These companies—including the Texas Delta Land Company, Kirby Lumber Company, and Long-Bell Lumber Company—collectively milled and treated hundreds of millions of board feet of local lumber every year. Americans wanted wood. Lots of it.[2]

The work was relentless and the destruction was undiscriminating. The depletion of white pines and hemlocks in Pennsylvania eventually drove logging companies into east Texas, where cypresses and loblolly pines grew in abundance. Timber harvested in regions as distant as San Augustine, Texas, was sent downriver to towns as far south as Beaumont and Orange; from there it was shipped by schooner or rail to construction sites throughout the United States. Northern Texas counties expanded the reach of the industry by felling large copses of shortleaf pines, gum trees, and cedar. Much of this wood was turned into a green lumber called "rawhide"—so named because it looked like untanned buffalo or cattle hide. By 1880 Texas ranked seventh in the nation in logging, having produced $3.5 million from "300,000,000 board feet of lumber, 14,000,000 laths, 100,000,000 shingles," and a variety of other products. Much of this raw material left the state in boxcars, but a considerable amount of it was used in Texas shipyards, as well as by regional carriage makers, coopers, and furniture manufacturers.[3]

One might reasonably conclude that this largely unfettered assault on southern forests would have spelled sheer disaster for the wild pecan groves that both Native American and (as we will see) white pioneers passively cultivated throughout the tree's native region. Indeed, there is every reason to speculate that in an era devoid of a powerful conservation ethic, the pecan should have fallen victim to the steady process of deforestation. However, that was not the case. For several reasons—all of them somewhat haphazard—the pecan tree yet again ran counter to the dominant flow of botanical history. With rare exception, the pecan avoided late-nineteenth-century deforestation in Texas and Louisiana and went on to thrive in the river bottoms that were so conducive to the growth of pecan trees. Given the trends of deforestation, it shouldn't have survived. But it did.

The most obvious explanation for the pecan's gritty persistence was, oddly enough, the pine tree. Pines offered better, faster-growing, and more accessible wood. Every pine tree in sight—loblolly, yellow, pitch, and longleaf—was quickly transformed by modern technology into plywood, planks, and sawdust. These products were then replaced with faster-growing pine seedlings ("slash pines") with the express intention of repeating the cycle within a couple of decades. Lumber companies built their empires on this tedious and nutrient-sucking process. The pecan, though, was not conducive to such clear-cutting and repropagation. As the pecan had a way of doing, it held its ground, thriving in the dense nooks of its native habitat and continuing to produce nuts, all the while immune to the fact that the South, much less the nation, was industrializing the American landscape with unprecedented speed. Indeed, the pecan paid little attention as the logging industry turned east Texas, as well as much of the American Southeast, into the veritable patchwork of a landscape that our current age has inherited—a region that bears witness to anyone who drives through it today to miles and miles of sclerotic slash pines separated by recently cleared patches of land.[4]

Lumber was not the only industry threatening the pecan's extensive presence in the American Southeast. Other commercial developments could just as easily have made things so a visit to an arboretum would be the only way to see a pecan tree today. By the middle of the nineteenth century, the Southeast as a whole, and Texas in particular, was in the midst of an economic and physical transformation of historic magnitude. Forests and grasslands were yielding to vast networks of intensive cotton and sugar plantations, corn and wheat fields. Livestock ranches of heroic proportions started to sprawl across the American South, reaching new orders of magnitude in south, central, and north Texas. "Early Texas settlers," writes one historian, "created, developed, and expanded agricultural landscapes and instituted a system of land ownership that allowed them to barter or sell plants, animals, and other resources from the land." The landscape, in essence, came to be seen and treated as "an assemblage of useful material objects."[5]

An 1858 report from New Braunfels, Texas, published in the *New Orleans Times-Picayune*, highlighted the hopeful promises these endeavors offered to white Americans willing to exploit resources on the Texas frontier. Noting with evident exasperation that Texas was "larger than New-York, Pennsylvania,

Maryland, Virginia, and Ohio put together," G. W. Kendall, a lawyer from back east, proceeded to nonetheless lionize the Lone Star State as a remarkable land of opportunity. Although Texas was poorly suited for raising sheep, with "the grass growing too rank and rich," there was no question that "for cattle and horses it cannot be surpassed." Especially helpful were the advantageous and abundant "cedar breaks," which blocked those "chilling blasts which scatter stock." Listing a dozen rivers, Kendall explained that "with proper tillage we shall always be able to raise more than corn and wheat enough for our wants." Cotton was not yet king in Texas, but even so, "heavy crops of it [are] made." The message couldn't have been more in tune with the prevailing spirit and rhetoric of Manifest Destiny. As one New York visitor to Texas in 1840 wrote to potential Texas immigrants: "Come on! As many as you wish. We will have enough for you all."[6]

The idyllic implication of western expansion rang crystal clear to many Americans seeking opportunity elsewhere: this distant part of the world was a yeoman's paradise. The water was clean, the borders were secure, the air was pure, the environment was "as healthy as any in the wide world," and even the children were said to be above average. Kendall and the anonymous New York transplant quoted above were hardly alone in promoting—mythologizing, really—Texas as midcentury America's promised land. Calls for migration echoed throughout not only the United States but the world. Tens of thousands—coming from locations as far away as Tennessee and Poland—migrated and, suffering and hardship and exploitation notwithstanding, attempted to do what the proponents of migration instructed them to do. Although plagued by disease, poor infrastructure, and hostile Native Americans, they worked to transform the land, carve out their space, and look toward a better future. Economic endeavors developed out of this passion, and with that development the landscape of Texas continued to change.[7]

As the South developed, cotton eventually did become king. It also became the second-largest potential threat, behind timber, to indigenous pecan trees in Texas. Cotton planters throughout most of the northern Mississippi River Valley typically extended their plantations all the way to the banks of rivers and streams—that is to say, to the very places that were so conducive to pecan propagation. A Little Rock, Arkansas, newspaper warned settlers against such relentless clear-cutting, espousing a balance between the quest for cotton and the preservation of native pecans. "A man who has 'cotton on the brain,'" it warned, too often cuts down all his pecan trees because "the trees take up too much good cotton land." At "ten cents a quart," the article (somewhat dubiously) continued, "pecans will bring twice the money that cotton would, and with no trouble of cultivating." The editors noted that pecans scattered along the Arkansas River were "bearing well" and, solely for economic interests, should be left alone by any landowner hoping to leave his children a modest but relatively labor-free inheritance.[8]

It appears, though, that few planters were willing to heed this advice—especially in the northern regions of the pecan's native habitat, where restraint was a rare commodity. Cotton was too tempting, too much in need of constant expansion, and potentially too profitable to leave room for even the thinnest fringes of dense pecan groves, however sensible the newspapers said it was to do so. As the *Arkansas Daily Gazette* lamented in 1870, "Only a few years ago our river bottoms were filled with fine pecan trees, which bore annually several bushels of nuts." Since then, however, "nearly all [have] been destroyed to make way for plantations." Other naturally productive and genetically diverse groves were allegedly "cut down by boys and negroes for the purpose of securing the yield of a single year" and then planting cotton.[9]

One gets the sense that—and again, we are talking about only the northern reaches of the pecan's habitat—something of a free-for-all was under way in this region. The commons were experiencing an all-too-familiar tragedy, and the pecan copses were some of the most vulnerable victims. Even the wanton felling of pecan trees undertaken to avoid the bother of climbing them and whacking down the nuts (or waiting for the nuts to fall) was not a rare event—although, naturally, any claim that it was undertaken exclusively by "boys and negroes" is rightly suspicious. As late as 1912, one writer recalled "the extravagant habits of cutting out the tops at harvest time and of chopping down trees altogether in order [to] more easily obtain the nuts." This practice, he added, happened "in many sections" of the region.[10]

But not in others. In the southern regions, especially Texas, pecans thrived as native specimens despite the expansion of the cotton economy, and despite the devastation taking place farther north. Indeed, as it turned out, while encroachment upon pecan groves for cotton and cattle was common in Arkansas, Kentucky, and southern Illinois, it happened rarely—very rarely, it seems—in Texas, Mississippi, and Louisiana. As the *Arkansas Gazette* article went on to report, "The pecan tree is indigenous to our climate and soil" and had the potential to "be made a source of much gain to our people as it is already to those of Texas."[11] Taking note of the wild pecan's secure purchase in Texas in 1892, the writer Walter Bigelow Stevens was duly impressed with the extensive and continued prevalence of wild groves. "Every water course," he explained, "has its fringe" of pecans. This was not happening in northern regions where the pecan grew wild, but the fact that pecan diversity was being purposely preserved in Texas and adjoining regions was quite important for the future history of this tree's remarkable genetic variance.[12]

Further evidence that pecan trees and Texas cotton peacefully coexisted comes from a typical 1889 account in the *Dallas Morning News*. Titled "Pecans and Cotton," this brief market report explained that "the pecan crop in this country is unusually large," adding in the same breath how "cotton has been coming in quite freely." Notably, there appeared to be no conflict over land appropriation between these two agricultural endeavors. Cotton fields and pecan groves not only coexisted but seemed to thrive together as interwoven aspects of the same commercial landscape. All of which raises a critical question: why? Indeed, why did Texas plantation owners not stretch their cotton fields to the river's edge, as did their counterparts to the north, thereby wiping out large portions of the region's wild pecans and turning the area into a homogeneous zone of monocultural production? Answering this question is critical to understanding how pecans in Texas and Louisiana went on to be passively cultivated, actively commercialized, and thereby made central to the future emergence of cultivated varieties, a coherent pecan industry, and the globalization of America's native nut.[13]

The answer has to do in part with quirks of hydrology and geography. Indeed, considerable evidence supports the claim that Texas and Louisiana planters were less likely to build plantations and clear pastures to the very edge of riverbanks. As a result, wild pecan groves, which were predominantly located along these edges, were more likely to be spared. The reason Texas farmers chose not to clear land along riverbanks primarily had to do with floods. Spring flooding was more frequent and intense in the southern portions of the pecan's native range. According to geographer William Keith Guthrie, proximity to the "moisture-rich Gulf of Mexico," "the low relief topography of the Great Plains" to the north, and the "long curving topographical discontinuity" of the Balcones Escarpment all combined to make the southern region where Texas pecans grew particularly prone to storms that induced large floods. These especially intense storms were seared into local memories and understood to be a necessary part of ecological life. In combination with the especially aggressive "human induced changes to the land," they further encouraged farmers and ranchers to avoid planting too close to riverbanks, where their tender crops would surely have been destroyed by the next inevitable surge. As a result, wild pecan groves, which fortuitously grew in these danger zones, were spared in Texas and Louisiana.[14]

Conveniently enough, wild pecans were also commonly known not only to survive mammoth floods but to thrive in them. "[I] have known water to cover the land around the trees three feet deep for a week," wrote one farmer, "without their showing any injury." As late as 1925, this phenomenon was still being observed and duly appreciated by farmers. "In Oklahoma," explained the *Christian Science Monitor*, "there are at least 160,000 acres of creek bottom lands overflowed at various times of the year," but "this overflow water has no effect on pecan trees other than to make them grow greater." More recently, a geographer observed how the pecan "has a competitive advantage over other bottomland species" because the tree "can withstand late-spring flooding." This was decidedly not the case with cotton and cattle—and it was therefore an important factor behind the pecan tree's survival during the era of cotton and cattle expansion and rapid environmental exploitation.[15]

Yet another explanation for the pecan's persistence and proliferation in Texas during a period of rapid and aggressive environmental transformation has to do with market proximity. As pecans evolved from a wild supplemental food source into a marketable commodity, there was considerable advantage in living closer to the three cities that were, for various reasons, becoming active nodes of agricultural distribution: San Antonio, Galveston, and New Orleans. Markets in urbanizing centers such as Little Rock, St. Louis, and Chicago were certainly significant, but they rarely exported pecans. To the contrary, they often imported them. However, the more southerly cities, surrounded by the world's densest pecan groves, supplied the nation with at least a sampling of wild pecans. In an age of precarious local transportation, being close to the markets where nuts could be shelled, packaged, and shipped was a keen advantage and, however indirectly, supportive of local pecan initiatives.

Import records of other cities confirm the point. As early as 1819, Providence, Rhode Island, was importing pecans from New Orleans; in 1825 a Philadelphia firm was advertising "PECAN NUTS . . . from New Orleans"; in 1874 pecans leaving from San Antonio and Galveston constituted the state's fifth-largest export; and by 1899 none other than Little Rock, located in the center of what had once been dense pecan land, was importing "pecans, Texas, polished." (Early pecan sellers polished pecans with varnish to make them appear fresher than they were.) To be sure, this trade was in its infancy, but, again, being near the key centers of export provided a certain incentive for farmers to preserve, passively cultivate, and transport wild pecans the relatively short distance to a vibrant market.[16]

Perhaps the most unlikely factor contributing to the persistence of wild pecans in Texas and western Louisiana involved pigs—or at least the decision to let them roam on their own. There is much to suggest that the citizens of Texas and Louisiana were more likely than those living in northern native pecan regions to allow domestic swine to live in a state of semi-domestication, feeding off the natural bounty of the backwoods, moving about at will. This decision was critical for the pecan tree, because one of the most substantial sources of nourishment for southern swine turned out to be scattered pecans, a factor that surely encouraged landowners to keep the trees standing. Writing in the 1830s, A. A. Parker, a farmer of modest means, explained how "hogs keep in good flesh all the year" primarily because "in autumn, when the nuts fall from the trees" they "grow fat." He described how "hogs can be kept in this country without any more trouble than merely looking after them to prevent their straying."

By the 1880s, the practice of allowing hogs to roam free through pecan groves remained alive and well. Oran Roberts, writing in 1881, noted how Texas swine breeders organized their breeding plans around expected pecan masting schedules. "When a good mast did come," he explained, "close attention would be given [the hogs], so as to raise a large number of pork hogs that year." Acknowledging how "this primitive mode of raising meat gradually gave way in most sections of the country," yielding to the increasingly common practice of "fattening them with corn," the author went on to confirm that Texas pig farmers held firm to a "dependence on masts for feeding swine." It was a habit, he claimed, "prevalent in most of the cotton growing portions of Texas." An 1873 newspaper account referred to "hard fisted farmers feeding [pecans] to swine," a decision that raised the price of pecans for humans but, alas, caused "no dispute between the [farmers] and the swine." As late as 1904, a state almanac could report on the common practice in Texas of "fattening hogs for market" with the use of pecans.[17]

A final explanation for the pecan's lasting presence in Texas (and Louisiana) centers on the fact that as it had been for Native Americans, the pecan was an excellent frontier food for pioneers. Texas had a comparatively long period of frontier expansion and development. Settlers were cut off for longer periods of time from systematic trade, transportation, and communication with the rest of the country. Much in the way that pecans served Native Americans as they developed a diet rooted in semi-nomadic wanderings, the nuts supplied Anglo-American settlers with subsistence calories and, in especially dire circumstances, a valuable means of exchange. An 1842 account from Austin revealed how "money of every description . . . has disappeared from this section," a situation that compelled citizens "to do business by barter, and take hides, pecans, etc. instead of money." Another observer of Texas's economic landscape in 1847 explained, "If the heavens do not rain manna in Texas" one could always rely on pecans for trade and sustenance. By the end of the century, an observer, speaking of the pecan tree, noted "what a golden layer the goose was." The author went on to chide Texans for taking this abundance for granted, adding that there were once "twice as many pecans as there are now," a comment that, in its lament, underscored the importance of pecans in local, barter-based, frontier-economy exchange. The reason for the decline, he explained, was the lazy habit of cutting down trees to acquire their nuts during times of scarcity, a shortsighted approach that, as we've seen, took place wherever the pecan grew.[18]

In the end, though, the bottom line was simple enough. As one choice piece of Manifest Destiny promotional literature noted, not inaccurately, "Millions of pecans grow wild in our forests." For a society holding firm, on at least some level, to a frontier ethic, this bounty was indeed a blessing. While relatively undeveloped landscapes gave way to commercial forces, the pecans in Texas and Louisiana held their ground against this onslaught.

If a wide variety of circumstantial factors—pine trees, flooding, swine, and the need for frontier food—conspired to ensure that Texas pecan trees remained "in boundless profusion" throughout areas of the Southeast, settlers themselves capitalized on the opportunities presented by this turn of events. Given what's been presented thus far, one might think that Anglo-American settlers did precisely what Native Americans had done—that is, basically pick up pecans where they fell and work annual harvests into the daily cycles of life. This they certainly did. Unlike Native Americans in Texas, however, white landowners between 1850 and 1900 nurtured pecan groves through passive cultivation. To be clear, they did not (with rare exceptions) plant orchards. What they did do, however, represented a crucial step in that direction. Basically, passive cultivation meant identifying thick patches of preexisting wild pecan growth, thinning out the competition, managing the pecan trees to favor the stronger and more productive individuals, and then allowing the groves to flourish on their own terms. Again, passive cultivation was not actually orchard keeping (that was indeed coming), but insofar as farmers channeled nature to serve human interests, it was a carefully calculated way to maximize pecan production without becoming actual pecan farmers burdened with the considerable task of managing formal and genetically narrowed orchards. So prevalent and successful was this method in Texas and Louisiana that even after the turn toward cultivated orchards with improved varieties in the twentieth century, there were always some farmers who continued to pursue the fine art of passive cultivation with, as we will see, beneficial consequences for the industry as a whole.

Here is how a pecan manual published in 1896 by the USDA Division of Pomology described the process of passive cultivation: "Numerous efforts have been made to clear up native groves by cutting out trees of inferior pecans and other timber, leaving good pecan trees as thick as they ought to stand for good crops." Another popular manual wrote about owners of "pecan-producing forests" who were increasing their productivity by "a careful and systematic elimination of all unprofitable trees, so as to give greater advantage to superior nuts." It warned that "clearing too suddenly will expose the remaining trees to injury by high winds." Gradual clearing, by contrast, will help in "converting the forest into an orchard." Ultimately, this was precisely the goal of passive cultivation—to convert the forest into an orchard—or at least something approximating it. Texas pecans were soon living in a state somewhere between the wild and the sown, which was not such a bad place to be, as it conferred higher yields while maintaining genetic diversity and, in turn, healthy trees.[19]

Examples on the ground show that this passive form of conversion became the nineteenth-century norm throughout Texas. A landowner in central Texas who maintained a native pecan grove noted that the cost of "converting" pecan banks to a pecan grove was "so small as to scarcely deserve a name." A visitor to Weatherfield, Texas, in 1877 observed the passive cultivation of pecans, noting "pecans on the creeks" that were thriving in the absence of other species. Another traveler to Texas in 1844 provided a more detailed description of a passively cultivated grove of pecans. "It seemed impossible to me," he wrote, "that nature, left to itself, could be so incredibly clean." He went on: "I involuntarily looked about to see the hand of man, of the artist, but I only saw a herd of deer."[20]

Naturally, the hand of man was present, but the touch, as the visitor suggested, was light. Indeed, it was the comparative ease of passive pecan cultivation that appealed to so many landowners who managed wild groves from western Louisiana to central Texas. It was the fact that one could, if fortunate enough to own land stocked with patches of wild pecan trees, turn them into a profitable natural resource with comparatively little effort that inspired so many Texans to selectively protect and propagate the tens of millions of pecans in their midst. As a newspaper columnist aptly put it, pecans, unlike apples or plums, were able to "yield amazing quantities of fruit without care or cultivation." And that, perhaps more than any other factor, was the key: this was work that could be done without care or cultivation.

This critical aspect of the pecan economy was well appreciated by labor-strapped Texans trying to fashion an economically stable life on an often unaccommodating frontier. After listing a range of fruits that required careful attention, the attorney G. W. Kendall commented on the pecan's ability to produce abundantly with minimal human input. "Where this nut grows," he wrote, "there is little need of any other—it is the best of all." "With comparatively little trouble," one newspaper explained, "extensive groves of these trees could be cultivated." A contemporary assessment of today's many pecan cultivars notes that "for 150 years growers have managed and harvested nuts from pecan 'groves' found throughout the tree's native territory." An Arkansas farmer in the 1850s was able to harvest pecans from several passively cultivated groves, travel to Fort Smith twice a year, and return loaded with "sugar, coffee, and other supplies." Again, this situation was much more common in southern rather than northern climes—and it essentially defined pecan cultivation, if not the entire "industry," for more than half a century.[21]

Cultivation may have been passive, but the gathering of nuts was anything but inactive. Harvesting pecans could be a contact sport. Eager to beat the competition and acquire pecans before supply increased and prices dropped, farmers sent their children scrambling into the pecan groves to scale trees and strafe nuts from precarious limbs. Needless to say, this activity precipitated its fair share of newsworthy mishaps. "Judging by the number of boys injured while picking pecans," opined the *Galveston News*, "it is fair to presume there is only one way to fall out of a pecan tree." In 1902, a teenage girl living in the Texas Hill Country decided to get a jump on the competition by rising into a pecan grove in a hot-air balloon, as a group of men held her in place with an anchor rope. She rewarded them by sending down, as she put it to the *New York Times*, "a shower of gold."[22]

Harvesting nuts from the ground, though, was a big enough deal to warrant mention in the local press, as it did when the *San Antonio Express* reported that "nuts were gathered from some large trees on the edge of the San Marcos bottom." Pecan poaching was not uncommon. When a boy was caught helping himself to pecans from private property during harvest season he quickly found his backside peppered with buckshot, a response that left him nursing what the paper deemed "painful but not dangerous wounds." The account of a missionary mentioned how "the banks of the Guadaloupe were strewed with Pecans, and very many were the persons, male and female, old and young, who went out to gather them." The man continued, "The pecan crop, once in three years, is a great affair in Texas," equal, he ventured, "to the cotton crop."

With good reason, observers often associated the pecan harvest with German immigrants. "The pecans were gathered at the Concho," reported the San Antonio paper, "by some Germans from Fredericksburg." An 1848 account in the *Houston Telegraph* noted, "We understand that many of the German emigrants at the west are realizing greater profits by gathering pecans than they have realized in their harvests of grain." This involvement was somewhat prophetic. As we will see, these German immigrants became central to the promotion of the pecan as an improved commercial crop later in the century.[23]

All this mad scramble for nuts produced by passively cultivated groves was not purely for the pleasure of experiencing the pecan's rich flavor. The wild pecan was slowly becoming a niche commodity as a direct result of passive cultivation, and Texas—which was endowed with the most pecan trees—was becoming the thriving epicenter of that commodity. Market reports in several southern papers offer ample evidence of this transition, one that would provide the basis for the expansion and technological transformation of pecan culture from a scattered and disorganized activity into a scientifically driven, consolidated, and eventually global industry by the following century.

The 1850s marked the early stages of this trend toward

commodification. Again, the widespread and decentralized habit of passive cultivation was the underlying cause. From Galveston, exports were 1,525 bushels in 1850 and 13,224 in 1854. An 1856 article from the *Texas Gazette* reported that local accounts from "the Colorado, the Guadaloupe, and the San Antonio represent the pecan crop as quite abundant this season." As for the Medina River basin, "it is said that [the pecan crop] will be larger this year than at any former season." A report from Georgia noted that "before the war the small port of Indianola, Tex., exported as many as 100,000 bushels." Exports at the time were predicted to be worth $50,000 a year.

By the 1860s pecan markets had become even more active, especially in San Antonio, where the Civil War had previously strained or disrupted traditional trading networks. The *Express* noted in 1867: "Pecans are coming in quite plentifully, and from all accounts the crop is very heavy." Merchants were typically paying $2.75 to $3.00 per barrel, with those merchants known for "buying largely" singled out by name and actively courted by increasingly commercial-minded owners of pecan groves. Even smaller ports such as Port Lavaca could, in this active economic climate, record the exportation of 1,500 barrels in 1866.[24]

Supply and demand were carefully monitored by pecan growers and exporters alike. Subtle market shifts were duly noted. On October 30, 1867, an influx of several "cart loads of pecans" depressed the price of the nuts from $3.00 to $2.80 per bushel, a figure that recovered the next week (back to $3.00) when several wagonloads reached New Orleans for export. Two years later, pecan gatherers stormed San Antonio with bushel upon bushel just days after the newspaper reported that "three large wagon loads were shipped east by Merrit and Brothers," a prominent merchant house with extensive connections on the eastern seaboard. Occasionally a critical mass of groves would fail to mast, as in 1870, and considerable frustration and confusion would ensue. "A few pecans have made their appearance in market," the *Express* wrote. "But this year's crop is very small and inferior." This situation stood in contrast to 1869, a year that saw "plenty of pecans" produced. As the price of pecans in New Orleans spiked to an unprecedented $12 per bushel due to a short supply, the *Express*, lamenting "the scarcity of the crop in Texas," wondered, "Will not some one who understands the matter account for the non-yield this year?" It may have been a bad year, but it wasn't permanent. By 1889, the *Dallas Morning News* was noting that "about 55,000 pounds of pecans have been sold in this market this season."

Whether the market for pecans was bullish or not, the important point here is simple: there was a market for pecans that showed no sign of abating. Texas merchants—and not just scratch farmers keeping groves for sustenance and barter—were beginning to see pecans less as a convenient local snack or the ideal frontier food and more as a supplemental cash crop. Taste for pecans led to a taste for cash and, as it did, the cultivation of a small market economy for pecans spelled a future for pecans based on higher productivity, higher kernel density, and increasing market share. Producer interest in these qualities was critical in helping to open the farmer's mind to the idea of active rather than passive cultivation.[25]

In an era of passive cultivation, Texas—again, with the natural advantage of having more wild pecan groves than any other state—would dominate the industry. By the end of the nineteenth century, Texas remained the unofficial center of pecan production—almost exclusively because of the harvesting of passively cultivated wild pecans. Between 1850 and 1900 the state went from a place where native pecans were a supplement to a frontier diet to a place where pecans had become a profitable commodity gathered from the region's extensive network of creeks, streams, and riverbanks. The primary mode of cultivation remained passive, gathering and marketing took place on a small, decentralized scale, San Antonio served as a commercial epicenter of sorts, and the nuts coexisted peacefully with cotton and cattle. Large pecan farms—actively cultivated with a narrow range of improved varieties—might have been foreordained from the moment a market formed for this crop, but they were still in the distant future. Even as late as 1899, formal pecan orchards were so few and far between that pecans ranked well behind walnuts and almonds in overall output. They ranked, in fact, dead last among all American-grown nuts.[26]

Still the situation in Texas foreshadowed a rise in the ranks for cultivated pecans. "The Pecan," according to a Dallas area farmer, "grows wild upon the valley lands along the streams; also upon the hillsides and heads of streams. Large quantities are shipped out of the state. Many thousands of bushels go to the northern states each year." As the pecan became increasingly popular among consumers throughout the United States, and as passive cultivators began to make more money from their pecan crops than their cotton crops, enterprising farmers elsewhere—often farmers with an interest in scientific farming—began to take a closer look at the pecan. Specifically, they started to think about being less passive in their efforts to promote the growth of the pecan crop. They began to wonder why the pecan shouldn't become like the apple, pear, or plum. Why not get more aggressive and systematic in controlling the output and kernel content of this delicious nut, making it more adaptable, more productive, fatter, meatier, and easier to extract than ever before? Why not improve upon nature and, perhaps, make even more money in the process?

Antoine's Graft

THE BIRTH OF THE IMPROVED PECAN, 1822–1900

*The pecan stayed totally wild for a long time. While most of its fruit-*producing peers were being domesticated, the pecan avoided the meddling hand of man for centuries. Pecan trees not only benefited from their fortuitous location along flood-prone riverbanks in Texas and western Louisiana, but produced just enough edible nuts under natural conditions for farmers to justify passively propagating them for the purposes of commerce and subsistence. The consistency with which farmers undertook this work was impressive—recall the modest market that formed in Texas by midcentury. Nonetheless, in staying so close to home, the pecan belied a major botanical trend of the time. It proved itself yet again to be a renegade member of the plant kingdom.

Whereas the sixteenth and seventeenth centuries were eras of botanical wanderlust, the nineteenth century, especially the latter half, was an era of progressive and scientific agriculture. Agriculturalists were becoming less concerned with discovering alien plants and more concerned with controlling the precise details of plant development. If there was one word that was used more than any other in the agrarian literature of the day, it was "improvement." Virtually every edible crop was being sculpted and chiseled and manipulated—primarily

∾ 50 ∾

through some form of breeding and grafting—into improved and more marketable varieties of the plant. A small but growing cadre of farmers, extension agents, and plant breeders nationwide worked incessantly to narrow the genetic diversity of fruit crops into select varieties that were higher yielding, more resistant to disease, easier to pick, pack, and ship, and more tolerant to drought or frost (but never, interestingly enough, more nutritious). Fruits and vegetables began to come with names, such as the Early Cortland apple, the Chinese Cling peach, and the Early Golden plum.

These efforts—as a stroll through any modern grocery will attest—eventually led to dramatically more abundant, tastier, and shapelier commercial pears, plums, peaches, walnuts, squash, and apples—fruits that were now capable of thriving under a multitude of conditions and in a multitude of microclimates. Although the genetic stock of these fruits and vegetables was being distilled into a set number of varieties, never before had consumers enjoyed access to so many choices of high-quality plant food. For the most part, plant breeders and their emerging infrastructure of agricultural support—mainly in the form of the USDA—were ultimately the ones to thank for this unprecedented explosion of improved varieties adapted to a wider range of geographies worldwide. It is popular in these days of endless reverence for the rugged individualist to condemn big government for its meddling in the business of doing business, but for nineteenth-century agriculture in the United States, big government made the diversification and abundance of healthy produce a daily reality.

Historically speaking, the concerted emphasis on improving fruits such as apples, pears, plums, and peaches made perfect sense. In their wild state, these fruits were commercially inadequate, if not virtually inedible. For whatever reason, though, something about them in their undomesticated form sparked human interest in their transformation. Their potential to become a crop was evident, albeit dimly, to some person, group, or, most likely, animal. Eventually, as interest grew and as the edible promise of the plant emerged, these chosen weeds evolved under the hand of human selection into crops. Indeed, their long-term popularity was the result of extensive and ad hoc human intervention through such techniques as seed selection, budding, and grafting, as well as agricultural refinements like soil enhancement, synthetic fertilizers, pest control, and irrigation. The history of agriculture is the history of these bit-by-bit ongoing efforts to tame, shape, and conquer plants that once grew wild but had to be increasingly tamed in order to offer a diversity of predictable foods to a growing population.

In its wild state, however, the pecan remained immune to such efforts until the late nineteenth century. This was much longer than any other native edible plant, highlighting yet another aspect of the pecan that makes it an exceptional commodity. Unlike so many other popular fruits, the wild pecan could remain edible on its own terms for hundreds, even thousands, of years longer than its counterparts because it is intrinsically pleasing to the human palate. The significance of this factor should not be overlooked. Throughout the nineteenth century, when farmers were actively improving fruits and planting orderly orchards of fruit trees, and thus rendering these crops directly and exclusively dependent on human management, the pecan—as a result of its natural edibility, relative abundance, and ease of extraction—continued to stand tall on its own terms. It was passively cultivated to achieve commercial viability, but its genetics were not commandeered and streamlined to the point of dependence. This was yet another aspect of this remarkable tree that placed it in a league of its own, allowing it to escape the full grasp of agricultural science longer than any other commercial fruit or nut crop in the history of American plant life.

Consider, by way of contrast, the peach. In its wild state the peach— imported to North America in 1747—is certainly edible. But it is also a bitterly acidic fruit—possessing nothing like the sweetness and juiciness one associates with it today, and certainly not, in its natural state, a plant poised to become a commonly consumed item. The Chinese began to cultivate these small, astringent fruits as early as the tenth century BC, and in time peaches became delicacies fit for the ruling elite. During ancient times the peach—which had now benefited from thousands of years of selective breeding—was introduced to India, where it reached a much wider audience of consumers. Eventually, Alexander the Great imported a few peach samples to Europe, and by the sixteenth century, the Spanish and French were hauling bags of peach stones to the New World, where Euro-Americans grew them in neatly kept orchards. This migration and transmutation was made possible, in large part, by slow and steady human-directed improvements—changes that made the peach more adaptable, available, accessible, tasty, and capable of long-distance travel. The aggressive hand of humanity was essential throughout.[1]

When we associate peaches with Georgia or South Carolina, or when we appreciate the peach as a staple summer fruit, we must not forget this history. The only reason the peach grows in Georgia or South Carolina (or Connecticut or California, for that matter), and the only reason I can walk to the nearest grocery store and buy one right now, even if I am in Idaho, and the only reason it will taste good is that it has been aggressively manipulated by humans to adapt, migrate, and thrive in a wide array of climates and conditions. In its native state the peach was an interesting little weed, and effectively useless, at least when it came to the human diet. As an improved crop, though, it became wildly popular, and remains so to this day. This background is well worth considering the next time we hold up a perfectly round and juicy peach and deem it "all natural." It is, after all, as natural as a baseball (and, if harvested too early, might taste like one).

The story of the peach provides a useful contrast to help us understand the late-nineteenth-century pecan. When the Chinese were bringing the ever-improving peach to India, and as Alexander the Great was introducing it to Europe, and as Europeans were hauling it to America, the pecan—which, recall, was treated by the Indians as a forage-able (rather than commercially marketable) crop and rejected by the Europeans as too close to the walnut to cultivate—remained rooted in its native habitat, generally unchanged as an integral and natural and inherently edible component of an indigenous, semi-nomadic diet. Remarkably, this remained the case all the way through the late nineteenth century, even after Anglo-American commercial agriculture came to dominate the colonized landscape and passive cultivation was increasingly (if unfairly) deemed the desperate refuge of the uneducated cultivator.

The pecan was thus in an odd situation, one that raises questions. Why this multi-thousand-year period of stasis for the pecan in the midst of constant agricultural change for crops such as the peach? What accounts for the pecan's longevity in a state of relative wildness? Why didn't farmers work to improve the pecan as they had the peach once its dietary and commercial value became evident? Obviously dozens of factors go into explaining the idiosyncratic botanical evolution of any crop, but the point here is this: the well-entrenched habits of foraging and passive cultivation obviated the need for "improvement." The pecan, in essence, was allowed to remain a wild plant for a much longer time than any other commodified fruit or nut primarily because its wild variety happened to bear fruit that tasted supremely domesticated. The long-term evolutionary arrangement between pecans and other forms of wildlife created fat and buttery nuts well before humans ever came along to discover them. Once humans did make this discovery, once they realized they wanted to eat pecans as an integral component of a standard diet, they were wise enough to agree that nature was doing well enough on its own with regard to pecans. Humans chose to encourage that process, nudge it along, but not dictate it. Given that every wild pecan tree had a unique genetic composition, this choice was a good thing, as that diversity protected the trees from insect damage and disease while still supplying an ample quantity of nuts.[2]

Eventually, of course, this balance would be upended. Demand for pecans—as well as commercial pressure to achieve bumper crops of them—would dictate more-efficient and more-aggressive methods of production. Today, as a result, the pecan is treated much as if it were a peach. It is this fact that ties back to our larger story. When the pecan joined the heady game of improvement—and it did so, as we will see, in hesitant fits and starts—the nature of the pecan, pecan cultivation, and the entire meaning of what it meant to grow pecans fundamentally changed. There are now hundreds of commercial varieties of pecans, all of them pioneered by expert plant breeders, most of whom worked during the first half of the twentieth century. Pecans have extended modestly beyond their native range, with the world's largest orchards stretching from South Carolina and Florida to New Mexico and California. Georgia and New Mexico—neither of which have native pecans—are the largest producers of pecans today. The Chinese consume more pecans than any other nation. To be sure, compared to other global commodities, the pecan continues to flourish in the general region where it was born—relatively speaking, it remains a provincial crop—and there is no doubt that wild pecans remained extremely popular as the transition to domestication occurred. Nonetheless, by the late nineteenth century, the game of pecan production (and, in a sense, the essence of the pecan nut) had entered a new realm.

How this transition was effected—that is, how the process evolved from passive propagation in native habitats to active orchard keeping in and beyond native habitats—is a compelling story, one that will unfold over the next two chapters. Two basic points guide the narrative. First, once the means of improvement was established—that is, once it became clear that a pecan could be successfully grafted onto an improved specimen—it took a long time, at least fifty years, for skeptical farmers to accept and adopt this technological change in significant numbers. A variety of reasons accounted for their hesitancy. Second, once farmers did accept the fact that grafted varieties could profitably coexist with passive cultivation, it took a mere twenty years to accomplish with the pecan what it took more than two thousand years for the world to accomplish with the peach—that is, transform it from a predominantly wild fruit into hundreds of domesticated varieties. The beginning of this story involves more than simply the scientific process of grafting. It involves people willing to carry out that process—an unlikely cast of characters that includes a pottery maker from South Carolina, a Louisiana slave, and several German immigrants. It is to them that we now turn.

In 1822 an amateur potter from Edgefield, South Carolina, became momentarily interested in what he enthusiastically called "summer grafting." Grafting is a horticultural procedure whereby the vascular tissues of two plants are joined by inserting a tissue sample of one tree into another tree in order to create genetically uniform canopies with desired traits achieved through asexual propagation. The scion—the tissue from the donor tree—is fused into the stock, or the recipient, leading to the unification of distinct genotypes. The procedure was initiated by the Chinese thousands of years ago, picked up by European orchardists in the medieval period, and is employed by orchard keepers worldwide to this day. It is one of the most basic horticultural techniques in modern agricultural production. Without it our food supply, as well as the diversity of that supply, would be vastly diminished.[3]

The purpose of this union—which can also be accomplished through other forms of grafting called "budding" and "top working"—is to achieve a uniformity of traits. Farmers historically chose to graft because the seeds of desirable trees—say, trees with hearty root systems and abundant fruit production—do not "come true." That is, they do not produce seeds that yield replicas of the impressive specimen from which they came. For some woody species the problem could be overcome by propagating offshoots from the roots, an approach that worked for the domestication of figs, pomegranates, and olive trees. For other species—such as apple, pear, and plum trees—rooting did not work. The sole technology that led to the domestication of these species was, therefore, grafting. This was also the case for the pecan tree.[4]

The pecan was especially difficult to grow from seed for the purposes of commercial production. As a Texas A&M horticulturist wrote in 1922, "Few plants show such a wide variability as the pecan when it is reproduced from seed."[5] The consequences of ignoring this reality were obvious enough. Witness the account of a Florida farmer trying to start a pecan orchard in 1911:

> We have yet to find a single instance where the nut of a seedling tree was as indentical [sic] with that borne by its parent plant. Occasionally they are better, but the rule is that they generally are vastly inferior to the fruit produced by the parent plant. Hence, if an orchard of trees of the same habit of growth, prolificness [sic], regularity in bearing, uniform throughout, trees which will produce a crop of nuts uniform in size, shape, color and quality, is desired, do not plant seedling trees.

Scores of these seedling trees produce nuts but little larger than chin-quapins, and it is a fact which cannot be gainsaid that the seedling pecan, up to the time of fruiting, is an unknown quantity, after which it is too frequently a disappointment.[6]

Here we have the articulation of one of the early twentieth century's defining challenges for commercial agriculture: imposing uniformity on diversity for the purposes of enhanced production. The Florida farmer's frustration with the unpredictability of seedling cultivation is clearly evident. Needless to say, many a prospective pecan orchardist had his hopes dashed after planting a field of pecan seeds harvested from champion trees only to watch them produce an orchard's worth of gnarled, dwarfed, and unproductive trees mixed in with a few stars and a lot of average specimens. And that would be a ten-year error. Grafting, budding, and top working, however, enabled a farmer to bypass this experience. It allowed him to do something that is essential to successful commercial fruit production: create uniformity within his crop and, in so doing, reduce the problem of unpredictability. Agriculturally speaking, it allowed him, for better or worse, to join pecans to the rationalized agricultural economy of the twentieth century.[7]

Abner Landrum, whose interest in the hard clay beneath his feet led him to primarily embrace pottery, was almost a century ahead of his time in applying grafting techniques to the pecan tree. By suggesting that pecans (in addition to walnuts, figs, and persimmons) could thrive and be grown uniformly through the grafting of new and improved varieties, he aimed to extend an ancient practice to America's indigenous nut. Farmers, as mentioned, had been grafting for centuries, but, as far as Landrum knew, never with the pecan. As we have seen, there was little need for doing so—foraging was common, passive cultivation worked just fine, and the demand for something new had yet to materialize.

None of this really mattered to Landrum. Most likely, he was at heart simply a tinkerer. He was just a curious guy who wanted to graft a pecan.[8]

Whatever the motivation, Landrum made his case for pecan grafting in an 1822 article he wrote for a popular national agricultural paper called the *American Farmer*. The secret to successful pecan grafting, he argued, came down to the timing of it. Essentially, he urged that pecan grafting practices should take place in the summer rather than in the spring, as was common with other fruit. "I was induced to make this experiment," he wrote, "from the rationality of the theory; it having occurred upon the slightest reflection that failures in spring grafting might originate from the dissipation of moisture, by the drying winds peculiar to that season, before the sap of the stock [the root section of a grafted tree] acquires sufficient motion to furnish the graft with due nourishment."[9] The pecan in particular did very well under this theory. He explained, "I have, this summer, budded some dozens of the pecan on the common hickory nut, without a single failure as yet." His self-assessment of this accomplishment was unequivocal: "I made the experiment," he concluded, "and succeeded." And then his successful experiment, in essence, was forgotten.[10]

Landrum died in 1859, just as the nation's sectional debate was reaching a fever pitch. At the time, not a single pecan farmer, to the best of our knowledge, had picked up on Landrum's grafting advice. Not only did nobody respond to his article, but for decades the agricultural record is notably silent on the issue of pecan grafting. In fact, Landrum's discovery went so unrecognized that, in 1885, a citizen as well informed as Rutherford B. Hayes could write his Texas friend Guy Bryan to say, "The pecans . . . reached here today in excellent condition . . . I shall plant some of them," thus working under the common assumption that they would come true, or at least produce trees with superior nuts. The option of grafting evidently never crossed his mind. The reasons for this reluctance to pursue grafting as anything more than a hobby are basic enough: there were already millions of genetically unique pecan trees to passively cultivate, the commercial demand for pecans was too small to justify the time and expenditure of starting an orchard, and, quite possibly, it was simply more macho to run a ranch with cattle than to turn that land over to pecans. A cowboy was a cowboy, after all.[11]

Landrum, for his part, was otherwise occupied in a variety of enterprising activities. He seemed not the least bit interested in spreading the news beyond his short *American Farmer* piece. Not only was he, as his obituary noted, "a pioneer in the pottery manufacture of this state," but he was also engaged in, of all things, building "a suburban village" and publishing a journal dedicated to "the promotion of the most useful arts and sciences." Landrum the Renaissance man also spent considerable time ensuring that his pottery investments—large kilns and sawmills in particular—did not go to waste when he died. He did so by assiduously training his slave, Dave, not only to read and write but also to continue his trade. According to one modern account, Dave "became the best potter in South Carolina." (Whether or not Landrum's work with Dave had something to do with his overall view of slavery we can only guess. But we do know that when the Civil War started, Landrum the Carolinian slave owner openly sympathized with the Union.) Despite his short burst of pecan enthusiasm in 1822, he spent the rest of his life involved in other fascinating endeavors. He left the future of the pecan—and the many advancements that would occur with pecan grafting—for others to pioneer. His article was, it seems, the end of his short affair with the enterprise.[12]

Other tinkerers were certainly out there. Indeed, not everyone in Landrum's wake was working under the mistaken assumption that seeds would come true, or at least result in consistently superior trees. Even if they did not know about Landrum's graft or his obscure article, a few quiet pioneers were experimenting with the idea of pecan orchards stocked with varieties that were both uniform and carefully crafted to avoid the vagaries of local conditions. Many of their efforts came to fruition in Louisiana, where one Dr. A. E. Colomb, of St. James Parish, Louisiana, cut scions (buds and stems) from a particularly impressive pecan tree located on a sprawling plantation abutting the Mississippi River (on the Mississippi side) and grafted them onto several small pecan saplings. High expectations, however, were quickly dashed. The doctor's grafts all shriveled within two weeks.[13]

Dr. Colomb had the good sense to pass his scions on to a friend, Telesphore J. Roman, owner of the Oak Alley Plantation in Louisiana. Roman's plantation was about 1,200 acres, most of it planted in sugarcane. It was also situated on the Mississippi River, a position that provided easy access to New Orleans, where Roman kept a town house to oversee the marketing of his crops. Although small by the standards of Louisiana sugar plantations, Oak Alley was typical in that off in the distance from the big house, nestled behind tight rows of one hundred perfectly aligned live oaks, sat twenty-two small whitewashed slave cabins. Roman himself knew precious little about grafting techniques. However, in one of those rough-hewn cabins lived a slave gardener named Antoine, who did. And where Dr. Colomb failed, Antoine the slave gardener succeeded.

Slaves such as Antoine knew pecans well. Accounts by former slaves indicate that pecans were an excellent forage crop for plantation chattel, one that complemented a sort of frontier, even Native American–like diet. Slaves passively cultivated pecans as part of plantation subsistence. Georgia Baker, an eighty-seven-year-old woman who worked on a Georgia plantation, recalled, "Dere was allus plenty of pecans" for the taking. These nuts, gathered up from the fields, were complemented with "possums, rabbits, coons, squirrels." A Mississippi slave who foraged for pecans when enslaved eventually planted them on his own property, once he was free. "I got 'karns (pecans) all sot out on my place," he told an interviewer. "De ree-lief folks say I ought ter sell 'em, but shucks! We eats 'em." Lizzie Norfleet, another former Mississippi slave, recalled that "the yard was filled with pecan trees," the nuts of which complemented, yet again, "possums, coons, rabbits," and fish. These are just a few references to pecans found in recorded slave narratives. While they say very little about pecan cultivation per se, they do suggest that Antoine was hardly alone as a slave taking an interest in pecans, if only for the purposes of basic sustenance.[14]

But Antoine's interest, surely due to his role as plantation gardener, clearly went beyond sustenance. When Roman handed Colomb's scions to Antoine, the slave successfully grafted them onto sixteen young pecan trees located on the gentle slope of land between the Oak Alley mansion and the slave quarters. This quietly momentous event turned out to be perhaps the most important development in the entire history of pecan cultivation. It took place in either 1846 or 1847. These improved trees bore impressive nuts, so much so that Roman had Antoine graft 110 more trees in a big pasture abutting the river. This was an ideal spot, rich with alluvial soil and primed for rapid pecan growth. Antoine used the same scions as he had for the original 16 grafted trees. These new trees, too, thrived impressively and produced fantastic nuts. By the Civil War, there were thus 126 grafted trees on the Oak Alley planation, all genetically uniform descendants of that lone tree situated on the banks of the Mississippi—a tree that was, evidently, killed on March 14, 1890, in a thunderstorm.

When the Civil War ended, Roman sold his plantation. The new owner, burdened with higher labor costs, summarily cleared the pasture of Antoine's 110 grafted pecan trees in order to expand the production of sugar. This decision was made just when the trees were reaching "their most productive age and the nuts from them were selling from $50 to $75 per barrel." But no matter. Commodity prices ultimately determined what a farmer chose to clear and what he chose to plant. In the early 1870s, due largely to the high price of sugar, only Antoine's 16 original grafted trees remained rooted in Mississippi soil, destined, one might have guessed, to fade into irrelevance.[15]

The plantation, however, was sold yet again. The new owner of Oak Alley was a German immigrant named Hubert Bonzano. Bonzano left Antoine's original sixteen pecan trees in place after he purchased the property—by now the unlikely global center of pecan experimentation—in the early 1870s. Bonzano (who had also "identified with the Union sentiment") typified the perseverance of so many immigrants to the United States. He moved to Louisiana in 1845 and delved into the ample opportunities offered to ambitious white men (no matter where they were from) by a rapidly westernizing nation. He held a variety of minor public offices—all elected positions—while serving as a voluntary administrator of Charity Hospital, a position to which he was appointed by the state's governor. He was a model citizen.

Bonzano's primary quest, like that of most of his neighbors, was to grow sugar and create wealth, a linked endeavor that focused his attention on his land, every aspect of it—including his trees. When he encountered Antoine's pecans, and found out where they had come from, he learned to appreciate the quality of the nuts they produced and, in turn, made some fortuitous decisions. Bonzano not only left the trees alone, but also took steps to make them known beyond his plantation.[16] He applied to exhibit Antoine's improved pecans at the Centennial Exposition, held in observance of the nation's hundredth birthday, in the then booming city of Philadelphia. This event was a vibrant celebration of American innovation and Bonzano's choice to showcase the fruits of Antoine's labors there changed the history of pecan cultivation, leading not only to several awards but also to an official name for Antoine's grafted improvement: the Centennial. History leaves no record as to the former slave gardener's location—or whether he was even alive—when the nuts from the tree he grafted were praised by the nation's leading agricultural experts for their "remarkably large size, tenderness of shell, and very special excellence."

The fact nonetheless remained: the Centennial became the nation's first improved, marketable, and widely disseminated pecan variety. Hundreds of other varieties would follow, but the Centennial led the way. As the Department of Agriculture noted in its 1904 Yearbook, "The Centennial is the first variety of pecan that was successfully propagated by budding or grafting. It was also the first variety planted in commercial orchard form, with a definite view of producing nuts for sale." The text went on to describe the varietal's signature qualities in the following terms:

Size large . . . form long, compressed cylindrical, gradually tapering to a wedge shaped apex; base conical, color bright grayish brown with rather scanty purplish splashes toward the apex; shell rather thick, partitions thin, cracking quality medium; kernel clear . . . of delicate texture and flavor, quality very good.[17]

Gates of change had opened for the pecan, which had finally, if only modestly, joined the ranks of grafted fruit. We must not forget that the wild pecan would continue to maintain many advantages, including reduced production costs and genetic diversity, but the improved pecan was now on the innovative pathway that the peach, the apple, and the plum had followed. As indicated, hundreds of other pecan varieties, each endowed with its own quirks and characteristics and, eventually, name, would follow. But the Centennial set this process in motion. The Centennial created a new course for pecans, pecan trees, and the American diet—eventually even the global diet—because the Centennial allowed growers to impose uniformity on diversity, predictability on chaos, commercialization on what had heretofore been a mostly foraged food.

The only reaction we have from Bonzano about the remarkable success of the Centennial was a brief "letter to the editor" he wrote to a Philadelphia paper that had reported on the grafted pecan nut's impressive performance at the exhibition. Bonzano's message could not have been more unexpressive or perfunctory: he wrote for the sole purpose of correcting the spelling of his name. Back in New Orleans, though, he was all business, pushing his product at every turn, aggressively marketing the Centennial through a variety of venues. He hired his friend Richard Frotscher, who was yet another German immigrant, to help him spread the word about the Centennial throughout the South. Nobody was better qualified to do so. Frotscher was a well-known merchant and a credentialed horticulturalist (the Royal Horticulture School in Leipzig) who, after initially migrating to Pennsylvania, came to New Orleans to start a small nursery business. Throughout the 1870s and 1880s Frotscher's advertisements for new and improved seeds and seedlings appeared weekly in southern newspapers. His well-regarded book *Gardener's Manual for the Southern States* became a standard reference manual for professional and amateur growers alike. He was eager to help his friend.[18]

Horticulturalists and nurserymen were perhaps the biggest champions of grafting, for obvious reasons: grafted trees were critical for their business. Frotscher wanted to make money. Still, his enthusiasm for the Centennial was strong, so strong that not only did he promote it, but he spent considerable time educating consumers about the art and science of grafting, budding, and top-working pecans in order to pioneer other improved varieties. The idea was this: growers who were skeptical of grafted varieties (and most were) would, if they embraced improvement, have more choices and more flexibility than ever before. Eventually, Frotscher was so taken with improved pecans that he even created his own pecan varietal: Frotscher's Eggshell. It became a moderately popular variety. "The variety," remarked one analysis of the nut, "is precocious, productive, and succeeds over a wide range of country." Given Frotscher's reputation, the description seemed apt.[19]

By the early 1890s, it was not uncommon for popular agricultural manuals to cautiously tout the virtues of several pecan varieties that were improved. William P. Corsa, author of *Nut Culture in the United States*, advised, for example, that "trees be always budded or grafted with varieties that are known to bear regular crops of large, well-shaped nuts."[20] Sound as this advice was, though, it has to be placed in context. Specifically, we must be careful not to assume that as a result of Antoine's graft and the promotional efforts that followed, the pecan industry promptly abandoned passive cultivation, favored this new agricultural technology, and charged into the twentieth century. Turns out nothing of the sort happened. Instead, what did happen—for very good reasons—was about fifty years of resistance, skepticism, and foot-dragging by farmers loyal to the allure and security of tradition, comfortable with the place they had carved out between the wild and the sown, and eager to stay there.

Despite the innovative and entrepreneurial efforts of men such as Antoine, Bonzano, and Frotscher—not to mention scores of unnamed extension agents, national agricultural publications, and plant breeders—the transition to large, homogeneous, tidily maintained orchards with consistent commercial production value was more evolutionary than revolutionary. This gradual, often fitful, transition is consistent with scientific and technological change in general. Still, it is noteworthy that for a half century after Antoine's graft, Bonzano's awards, and Frotscher's promotion, pecan farmers throughout the South responded to the clarion call for "improvement" with a noble quality not uncommon in the agricultural trenches: doubt. For all the excitement in Philadelphia, reactions in the fields were characterized by a suspicion of outside "expertise," an adherence to tradition, a preference for piecemeal change, an appreciation of the low costs of passive cultivation, and, most importantly, a desire to manage agricultural change on the local level. Future pecan orchardists would graft when they were ready to graft. No sooner, no later.

While it is fair to say that the Centennial ultimately changed the way pecans were grown, and it's equally fair to say that all pecan improvement owes its existence to the horticultural talents of a slave gardener, it is just as important to note that this change was slow to take off, no matter what the experts were advising, and that pecan growers had excellent reasons for not grafting.[21] A 1912 USDA publication succinctly captured the prevailing climate of suspicion among everyday pecan growers. "The pecan," it declared, "must be done by asexual methods of propagation, i.e., by grafting or budding." So the word was out, but few were listening. The report continued, "In contradiction to this [advice], certain tree dealers have recently advanced the claim that grafted and budded trees are proving unsatisfactory, asserting that they are shorter lived and more subject to disease than seedlings; that they are otherwise objectionable and are being discarded."[22] The claim that seedlings were more resistant to disease was likely correct, as the genetic diversity of seedlings would have offered the trees more protection than trees asexually propagated. Nonetheless, the report bristled at the claim. "Evidence to support this claim," it huffed, "is entirely lacking." The very fact that such information was in circulation among farmers, however, meant that they would be extra cautious about abandoning something as simple as planting a seed for something as complex as grafting a seedling, or, even more threatening to one's independence, purchasing one from a nursery. Autonomy, or at least the perception of it, was critical to these farmers. With the advent of pecan grafting, a quiet rift thus formed between agricultural scientists and farmers. Bridging this divide—and how to do so—became a matter of the utmost importance.[23] In a sense, as we will see in the next chapter, an information war was taking shape.

From the pecan growers' perspective, there were powerful forces working against the adoption of grafted trees. For one thing, the startup costs were substantial because it took ten years for the returns to flow in from grafted varieties, assuming they turned out to be healthy. Doubling this risk was the fact that farmers would be forgoing returns from wild pecans at the same time, since labor and land would be consumed by the grafts. In addition to this economic factor's mitigation against the adaptation of grafting in native regions, there was very likely a subtle cultural issue in play as well. Farmers who were passively cultivating pecans were doing so as a supplemental endeavor—usually raising cattle was their main business. It is not beyond the realm of possibility that men whose primary occupation was raising cattle were hesitant about the gender and status implications of trading in the title of cowboy for that of pecan orchardist.

These considerations notwithstanding, one factor that did nudge growers to think about embracing improved varieties was the potential to expand pecans beyond the native range. Many manuals at the time explained that if the soil was right and the seedlings were hardy, geographical expansion of the pecan to areas where it traditionally did not grow (such as inland areas) was quite possible. According to a 1902 publication, planters could plant "in almost any kind of soil" if there was proper fertilization and irrigation. An interesting trend developed on the back of this advice. During the second half of the nineteenth century, when grafters, tinkerers, and gardeners such as Antoine and Frotscher were actively improving pecan trees to enhance uniformity and yield, there emerged a tendency among agriculturists to move with caution into new territory, primarily by experimentally planting pecans in places well beyond their native locales. Growing their crop in non-native locations encouraged pecan farmers to grow with non-native seeds—seeds that were likely to do well in unfamiliar soil. Fertilizers and irrigation might nurture wild seedlings for a while, but eventually these growers became a cohort that would be more open to grafts than were those farmers working wild pecans on native soil. New land needed new seed, and farmers on that new land, not surrounded by wild pecans, were more inclined to try them out, even if only experimentally.[24]

Enthusiasm over the mere possibility of bringing pecans to non-native regions of the United States picked up steam during the latter decades of the century. This willingness to experiment with new seeds in new locales proved to be a prerequisite for adopting pecan improvement. Not that growers were going to risk substantial labor and land on such a venture—at least not initially. A California newspaper, for example, advocated planting pecans—but only along railroad lines. Not only could the trees "attain great size in a few years," but the presence of pecan groves would provide wood for fencing, nuts for eating, and shade "to modify the summer heats." If farmers grew "pecan trees along the Sacramento River," they could avoid importing hickory wood to build wagons, an expense that ran $100 for 1,000 feet of wood. Another California article praised "the practicality of growing hard timber on our treeless plains" (a very popular idea during the homesteading era) and urged in particular "the cultivation of the pecan tree." By 1922, the *Christian Science Monitor* could report: "Experiments made at California show that pecan trees will thrive there."[25] California had never seen a native pecan tree, but the idea of domesticated imports began to gain traction, if only on modest plots for experimental rather than commercial purposes.

It wasn't just the west coast that was branching out into pecan cultivation. A report in the *Floridian* insisted (erroneously) that the pecan "grows as well [in Florida] as on the banks of the Mississippi," arguing (correctly) that it "can be made as productive as any crop in America." Thus pecans were moving into new territories by the late nineteenth century, with at least some vocal, if exaggerated, encouragement. The combination of nascent progress in pecan grafting during an era of agricultural improvement (with considerable governmental incentive to plant trees) and a growing consumer interest in pecans was indeed leading many farmers to expand pecan cultivation beyond the native habitat. As one newspaper urged: "Plant Trees," adding that the "farmer of today, considering the slight trouble and labor, can do nothing more certain to return a rich yield than to plant in fence corners and waste places, walnuts and pecans by the thousand."

The reasoning seemed to be that if these samples planted in non-native places took root, then it might make sense to undertake a more direct effort to plant and manage orchards with more-expensive and improved varieties. This was a natural and perfectly sensible progression. An obvious connection existed between the willingness to plant pecans in non-native regions and a willingness to plant improved varieties. This connection may very well explain the observation of one modern assessment of the pecan that "improved varieties of the pecan have been developed commercially in states east of the native pecan belt, rather than where they are native."[26]

Nowhere was the enthusiasm for early pecan expansion and experimentation more evident than in Georgia. Before the arrival of improved varieties, not a single native pecan ever grew in the state. In 1887 a Macon newspaper reported on "testing the home raised pecan nut grown on the place of Mrs. F. E. Burke" and finding the samples to be "very much superior in taste and flavor to the imported nut." From Gainesville, Georgia, in 1886 came the news that a Mr. F. Pfeffer "contemplates setting out several hundred pecan trees on his farm near town" under the assumption that "pecans will pay better than apples." Given the time required for trees to begin bearing fruit—about ten years—all eyes were on the future. "Within twenty or twenty-five years," the article continued, "a few acres of land so planted and well attended to would yield a fortune." Farther south, in Savannah, one Capt. W. W. Gordon produced pecan nuts that were "unusually large and fine flavored." The speculation based on Gordon's accomplishment was that "if good crops of such pecans can be raised in this latitude the growing of them would be quite profitable." Little did anyone at the time know how correct this assessment was. Today Georgia, growing exclusively improved pecans, is one of the world's leading producers of the nut.[27]

Agriculturalists did not limit this experimentation in expansion to regions similar in climate to Texas and Louisiana. They also moved into more far-flung and less geographically amenable locations, places prone to cold weather and hard freezes. Even if they did so in only a haphazard sort of way, their actions revealed an emerging national interest in planting an unfamiliar tree in unfamiliar locations. An 1896 publication, *Nut Culture in the United States*, identified "an orchard of 150 trees, about 7 years old, at Federalsburg, Maryland." The trees evidently showed "thrifty growth." In addition to the fact that "several persons in Delaware are growing a few trees," there was a seventy-year-old transplanted tree in Ohio that was "bearing good crops," as well as "40 or 50 4-year old trees making satisfactory growth" in Dansville, New York. Even more unlikely, there was the case of Robert Manning, of Salem, Massachusetts, who nurtured "a promising [pecan] tree, grown from a nut sent him from Illinois." Not surprisingly, all the seedlings that came from Texas nuts "have winterkilled as fast as grown." Still, the effort itself is worth noting. Assessing this nationwide habit of experimentation, the pecan expert William Corsa opined in 1893, "The pecan is probably destined to become the leading nut of the American market."[28]

As it turned out, Corsa was right. Once again, though, it is important to appreciate the halting nature of this transition in the wake of Antoine's graft and the Centennial's success. As noted, a centralized and coherent pecan industry did not immediately emerge around improved pecan varieties. It might be helpful to remember Max Planck's summarization of why scientific and technological change happens gradually: "a new scientific truth does not triumph by convincing its opponents and making them see the light, but rather because its opponents eventually die, and a new generation grows up that is familiar with it."[29] This assessment seems especially apt when it comes to the improved pecan. Pecan orchardists, after all, had a hard time leaving behind the habit of either passively cultivating pecans or growing pecans from seed. Repeatedly, progressive farmers and the USDA were still forced to point out the critical fact that pecan nuts do not come true, even as enterprising farmers were optimistically trying out pecan seedlings to establish commercial orchards.

The message was publicized in a variety of venues. The Division of Pomology recounted the case of a Louisiana pecan farmer who "sends us numerous specimen nuts grown from seed which came from a single tree that stood at least one fourth a mile from any other bearing tree." The result: "These nuts show a wide variation, none of them being alike, nor like the nuts from the parent tree." In case the lesson was missed, the report reiterated that pecan trees "can not be depended on to reproduce from seed." This information, in other words, was becoming abundantly available and consistently reiterated, but rarely followed in places where pecans grew wild.[30] The planting of choice seedlings continued to dominate—and it would do so well into the twentieth century. Considerable evidence demonstrates that despite the promotion and increasing availability of improved varieties in the latter decades of the nineteenth century, conventional pecan wisdom remained: plant choice seeds harvested from choice trees where one wanted an orchard to grow, if only to passively cultivate.

An 1870 report from Arkansas explained how "the pecan produces its good quality very generously by the seed." An 1874 Mississippi account noted how "the pecan is of the hickory family and is easily propagated by the nuts." Another letter from Arkansas promoted propagating pecan orchards from seed, observing, "the fruit can be sown almost broadcast." A Savannah report noted that "individual trees are found which produce nuts much larger and with thinner shells than the average." It was these nuts, it added, "that should be selected for propagation." In Texas, a prospective orchardist chose "large nuts with soft shells" and planted "where trees were to grow." The Centennial had been pioneered, marketed, and duly praised. Nonetheless, the simple act of planting seeds from desirable trees and hoping they bred true would not go gently. To this day, it remains common, primarily because it's beautifully simple, and works just often enough to completely discourage the decision to do so.[31]

Given this emphasis on growing seedlings, rather than grafting or buying grafted saplings, it comes as no surprise that discussions of agricultural matters, and of pecans in particular, often centered on specific trees that, in one way or another, were deemed outstanding for their size, duration, and, of course, seed quality. The *Galveston Daily News* praised a "tall and ancient pecan tree at Bonnet Carre Point, on the

Mississippi River that, forty years ago, furnished the supply of pecans that Monsieur Bernard de Marigny, of New Orleans, sent yearly to his former guest, the Duke of Orleans." From San Saba County, Texas, came news of a "pecan tree . . . the trunk of which measures six feet in diameter and a line drawn across its branches at the widest place measures one hundred fifty feet." A *Texas Monthly* article praised a tree in Toledo, Texas, that "averaged 500 pounds of nuts yearly." The message was clear enough. Prospective growers were urged to take note of these proud parents, plant their seeds, and await the brilliant results. Plant breeders and nurserymen, forlorn and frustrated, could only shake their heads in dismay, waiting for what they saw as agricultural enlightenment to take hold of the pecan and its bright future.[32]

The days of hunting and gathering were over. So were the days of exclusive passive cultivation. With grafting, humans and pecans were entering a new phase of their relationship, one simultaneously marked by ecological balance and impending disruption. The balance inhered in the relationship that was evolving between cultivars and wild varieties. The persistence of wild pecans in the midst of this incipient grafting transition had an unappreciated but undoubtedly positive impact on the overall health of the pecan tree. Not only did seedling trees continue to contribute substantially to the nation's supply of commercial pecans but, in all their sexually propagated genetic diversity, they decreased the chances that a disease might infect one genetically uniform variety, devastate it, and then jump to the next. In this sense, the wild pecans undoubtedly helped the cultivated ones. This same diversity also marked the impending change. It was, after all, the existence of vast genetic differentiation among pecan trees that enabled horticulturalists to take a found seedling and graft its scions onto other established wild pecans (or nursery stock) to ultimately drive the business and experimentation of grafting. As wild pecans were maintaining a tradition of genetic diversity and relatively seamless integration into native environments, cultivated ones were narrowing that diversity to create greater yield and uniformity. These qualities were essential for commercializing the pecan.

This is where matters stood on the eve of the century's turn. The pioneering work of a potter from South Carolina, a Louisiana slave, a couple of German immigrants, and a handful of nurserymen had led to the undeniable conclusion that the future of any viable pecan industry worthy of the name would be ultimately rooted in the science and technology of pecan production—namely, the use of improved varieties. However, innovation proved to be one thing, adaptation of that innovation another. Old habits die hard in agriculture and when it came to pecan cultivation, perhaps even more so. In native regions farmers continued to passively cultivate, as it was cheaper, easier, and less labor-intensive than clearing a field and starting an orchard from scratch. In places where farmers lacked access to native groves, they sometimes acquired seeds from the impressive trees that they read and heard about and planted them, working under the assumption that either those seeds would come true or they would at least create an orchard of above-average, if not entirely uniform, trees without the time and expense of grafting, transplanting, or buying from a nursery. These options made perfectly good sense. They did, however, inhibit the rapid transition that many—especially nurserymen and agricultural scientists—wanted to see happen.

There was also more than technology to consider. There were thornier and more personal matters—matters of pride, control, and independence. Farmers did not necessarily trust someone else's idea of "improvement." They wanted to know, for starters, if grafting was a procedure they could do themselves or if it would force them into dependence on nurseries and outside "experts." They had specific questions, very different questions from the ones asked by passive cultivators: Did one buy improved seeds and graft them himself or did he purchase grafted seedlings? Did one plant improved seeds where he wanted them to grow or start them in one place and transplant them to another? If one did transplant, did the entire taproot have to be removed? How far apart should one space orchard pecans? What variety of seed should one use? Could one plant improved varieties away from rivers? Before a pecan industry could emerge around Antoine's discovery, these questions would have to be answered. Farmers, moreover, would have to be the ones providing the answers.

These barriers to change were substantial—but not insurmountable. What happened in the upcoming decades (between 1900 and 1925) was the transformation of pecan growing into a consolidated industry with global reach. This consolidation was probably bound to occur, because with the advent of the Centennial a fundamentally new way of thinking about pecan cultivation had, however tentatively, taken root. As the Texan pecan farmer George Tyng put it in 1896: "No more costly mistakes have I made than in trying to follow nature in raising the pecan. Every agricultural success has been achieved by overcoming nature's effort to defeat it."[33] It would be on this ideology—an ideology that determined it was the human's job to direct nature as aggressively and authoritatively as possible—that the pecan industry would come to embrace the ethic of "improvement" during the first three decades of the twentieth century.

CHAPTER 5

"To Make These Little Trees"

THE CULTURE OF PECAN IMPROVEMENT, 1900–1925

Any doubts one might have had that grafting did not fundamentally change the pecan industry during the first quarter of the twentieth century would have been silenced by the numbers. The southern states that were the most aggressive in adopting improved—grafted, budded, or topped—varieties saw their share of cultivated pecan trees shoot skyward. Between 1900 and 1925 Alabama went from 25,000 orchard trees to 170,000; Mississippi from 40,000 to 710,000; South Carolina from 10,000 to 200,000; Florida from 39,000 to 524,000; Texas from 359,000 to 2,419,000; and, most dramatically, Georgia, from a mere 30,000 trees in 1900 to 2,368,000 in 1925. Overall, twelve southern states saw the production of improved pecans rise from 567,000 to 8,733,000 in just over two decades. It might have taken a while, but the logic of Antoine's graft had finally been embraced.[1]

During these years pecan production reached a tipping point. Eight decades of decentralized experimentation and pervasive doubt regarding systematic orchard keeping finally crystallized into a set of standardized procedures that provided the technological foundation for a powerful agricultural industry. Pecan grafting inched into mainstream commercial agriculture and, as it did, growers began "making trees" rather than passively cultivating them or planting them from seed. This chapter explores the intricacies of how and why this transition happened when and where it did.

If there was a single year that marked a decisive turning point from the systematic planting of pecan seedlings to the systematic propagation of improved pecan varieties, it was 1902. It is hard to say why that was such a critical year, but it assuredly had something to do with the convergence of several factors critical to convincing once and future pecan growers that it made little sense to repeat the same experiment without achieving measurable results. Indeed, there was little reason, despite episodic success with wild plantings, to plant orchards with seedlings that were bound to fail in producing consistent yields of high-quality, meaty, thin-shelled pecans. The point was now driven home by a chorus of powerful voices in the field of agricultural science: planting seeds and waiting until harvest season was a waste of time and agricultural space—a tired anachronistic behavior emblematic of a dark age long past—if one wanted to get into the pecan business in a real way. This was, of course, a belief framed by the concerns of high productivity rather than those of preserving genetic diversity.

Examples of this decisive shift in tone are confirmed in the three most popular pecan reports published that year—two of them government publications, the other from a prominent nurseryman. The first came from the Louisiana State University Extension Service, a publication that every pecan grower in the region would at least have heard about, even if he had not had direct access to it. This missive lamented that the habit of building orchards from seed had persisted far too long. "Men who desire the best pecans today," it declared, "do not follow this custom." Instead, they "bud or graft upon them the best varieties available." They undertook this procedure because, the report explained, "there is no other sure way of obtaining nuts which are known to be the most desirable." This message had certainly been outlined before, but never so bluntly, with such insistence and with such little tolerance for passive cultivation. It went on: "A person should not put any confidence in the statement of any nurseryman or tree agent who offers seedling trees of desirable pecans, for he cannot guarantee them to produce fine varieties, or even as good as the seed planted to produce them." The word was now made official. The Extension Service could no longer support in any way—not even as a last resort—planting seedlings as a viable commercial option. Grafting was the future. For anyone who hoped to make money growing and selling pecans, planting seedlings was not a workable part of the equation.[2]

The second report came from the USDA's Bureau of Plant Industry, following quickly on the heels of the LSU publication. It was even more direct in tone and less tolerant of traditional methods. In a section subtitled "Why the Pecan Should Be Budded," the author, George W. Oliver, reminded farmers how "seedlings from nuts of the choice varieties do not come true." In fact, "it would be remarkable were the seedling to produce nuts equal in size and flavor to those of the mother tree." Any farmer stubborn enough to pursue such a method in the face of current conventional knowledge was doomed to experience "a good deal of disappointment" if not outright ridicule from the reality-minded agricultural community. By contrast, there was an accessible alternative that the USDA could now fully commit itself to promoting. "Necessarily," Oliver wrote, "the only way in which the choice varieties of the pecan can with certainty be perpetuated in a manner to permit of being handled by dealers, is by budding or grafting on seedling stocks." Once again, the implication was basic enough—if farmers, southern farmers in particular, were going to prosper by selling pecans with uniform qualities, they would have to take charge and direct the shape of both their trees and, in turn, the industry as a whole. Nature, for too long, had called the shots, but nature did not follow the logic of mass production. Now, even though it meant more work and required learning techniques unknown to past generations, the farmer could gain the upper hand over wild pecan trees, turning them into genetically uniform commodities rather than honoring their wild side.[3]

The third report, a self-styled "Treatise on Pecan Culture," came from a nurseryman in Georgia named G. M. Bacon. Like the government reports, Bacon's treatise assured readers that improved varieties were the key to achieving industrial uniformity. He thus made his case in the strictest terms, writing, "Grafted and budded trees have advantages over seedlings because 1) they usually begin to bear much earlier than seedlings; 2) they reproduce the variety from which buds and grafts were taken; 3) uniformity in size, shape, and quality of nuts; 4) perpetuation of characteristics of parent tree; 5) greater care and attention usually given them on account of their greater value." This was the nurseryman's line, and there's certainly no doubt that Bacon had a personal interest in cultivating clients for the cultivated varieties peddled by his own nursery. However, Bacon also believed so strongly in the virtues of improved cultivars that he advised and even instructed readers who could not afford nursery samples to bud and graft themselves—something the vast majority of farmers would do, at least for a while. "It behooves everyone," he explained, "to have all seedlings converted into specific varieties."[4] Bacon believed in profit. But like so many others of the era, he also believed in grafting pecan trees to serve not nature's economy but the human economy.

These reports made something of an impact on pecan farmers. They were unique not only for the force of their opinions and the clarity of delivery, but also for the fact that they had genuine traction with readers who were in limbo on the grafting question. Keep in mind how many good reasons there were *not* to adopt improved varieties. A grafted orchard required a ten-year start-up period, considerable land taken out of some other form of production (usually cattle), and dependence of outside authority rather than the comfort of tradition. Understanding why growers responded so positively to the message of cultivation, in light of these drawbacks, is critical to understanding the history of the pecan tree. What was it about these reports, and the experts behind them, that suddenly made them appear trustworthy to the average farmer, a trust that could be built upon to gradually transform the pecan tree from a wild plant into a cultivated commodity? What factors tipped the scales of skepticism and encouraged common growers to pursue a strategy that would allow them to start building an industry with global reach on the back of consistent yields of uniform pecans?

We have already seen how pecan farmers resisted external expertise throughout the latter half of the nineteenth century, displaying a skepticism so persistent that most growers were still planting pecans from seed, or passively cultivating, well into the twentieth century (and the twenty-first). Similarly, we have also seen the popular appeal of maintaining groves through the techniques of passive cultivation, which involved minimal labor and could be pursued as a semi-profitable supplement to more permanent agricultural work. These were powerful mitigating factors working against the systematic adoption of cultivars. So, again, what was it about these three reports that allowed them to have such a dramatic impact on popular pecan planting? After decades of hearing about grafts, why, in the early 1900s, did pecan farmers finally turn the technological corner?

A general explanation might go something like this: Leaders in agricultural thought—namely, agricultural scientists and nurserymen—learned something very important. They learned that social relations determined technology transfer more directly than any objective account of that technology's effectiveness. In other words, the quality of communication between scientific expert and individual planter mattered more than the advertised objective benefits of grafting and budding. Experts learned the critical lesson that to have authentic influence on pecan farmers, they would have to work with them, rather than dictate from the high pedestal of expertise what the farmers should do to properly grow pecans. Additionally, it helped that the USDA and state extension agencies had been remarkably successful in a related endeavor, one that engendered considerable trust. This was an endeavor that also involved farmer-expert communication: controlling insect pests in other cash crops. The USDA had already achieved a big victory by 1900 on this front, and that precedent was one that farmers recognized and came to appreciate. They were ready to build upon that success and apply it to pecan cultivation.

These factors worked together to help initiate a staggering 1,300 percent rise in pecan production between 1900 and 1925, launch an industry that continues to thrive to this day, and in the process fundamentally alter the very nature and meaning of that once natural entity known as the pecan tree.

Farmers were fiercely independent. They were none too eager to have scientists dictate their behavior. They were none too eager to have *anyone* dictate their behavior. Central to the task of overcoming the suspicion that farmers instinctively harbored against outside agricultural authority, therefore, was the need to work closely with farmers themselves. They had to be empowered and emboldened. They needed a voice, especially if they were going to take the risk of becoming full-time pecan orchardists. Indeed, the necessity of including growers in the process of discovery was, scientists were coming to learn, a prerequisite for successful adaptation of any productive technology. Additionally, and perhaps more important, experts had to assure farmers that no matter how complex the transition to an orchard of improved trees might be, no matter how time-consuming, the growers would always be in the driver's seat. On these points, pecan experts—who, it must be reiterated, had a direct professional interest in the proliferation of improved pecans—made substantial progress. Pecan improvements, in essence, came down to personal politics.

Tactics varied. In a series of late-nineteenth-century reports explicitly intended to persuade farmers to adopt improved varieties, experts now chose to solicit firsthand information from the minority of pecan farmers who were early adopters of grafted varieties, rather than directly instructing all growers what to do. Readers of USDA bulletins could now learn from experimental but experienced pecan growers themselves just how well grafting and budding were serving their economic and agricultural interests. These testimonies, if for no other reason than that they came from real farmers, carried added weight with pecan growers who were otherwise wedded to maintaining wild stock. They also, if only implicitly, suggested to farmers that if they did not jump on the bandwagon of cultivation, their peers would quickly leave them behind. A little peer pressure in this respect could go a long way.

The rural voices promoted by the agricultural scientists were simple, trustworthy, rooted in common sense, and, most importantly, marked by experience. A New Orleans pecan grower explained, "In June and July, when the seedlings are very sappy, we take off a ring of bark about three-fourths of an inch long from the nursery stock to be budded and replace it with a ring cut from a branch of equal size on the tree to be propagated." He noted, "This is the best way to propagate pecans in this climate." From Ocean Springs, Mississippi, one John Keller reported and exalted in the fact that 90 percent of his budded seedlings were expected to flourish. E. E. Risien from San Saba, Texas, testified that he had "attempted to propagate the pecan by budding small seedling trees near the ground." "Experiments," he concluded, "were successful to a degree." From Kentucky, John G. Kline noted, "I have been successful in grafting on hickory [pecan] near the surface and hilling up to exclude air from the graft." From Florida a farmer reported of his grafting experience: "quite successful . . . I have 1,000 thrifty young trees." Such testimonies were gathered and presented to pecan farmers as meaningful evidence of progress, free of selfish ulterior motives.[5]

These reports constituted the quiet hum of progress as it transpired out in the orchards. They were pivotal in that they offered powerful examples of farmers talking to farmers through channels established and monitored by USDA experts. To reiterate, when it came to accurate agricultural information, how knowledge was spread was proving to be more important than precisely what was being communicated. In listening to these agricultural voices, in witnessing farmers talking to farmers, we get closer to an understanding of how pecans were tamed into thin-shelled, high-yielding commercial gems falling onto orchard floors across the southern landscape, uniform in size and taste, ready to be processed and shipped around the world.

Embedded in these accounts, moreover, were added assurances designed to appeal to skeptical growers. One aspect that stands out was a pervasive emphasis on flexibility. The perceptive agricultural reader would have been comforted by the wide variety of options that farmers employed to match particular solutions to particular problems. There was no rigid playbook that they were being asked to follow. Choice remained paramount. San Saba's Risien employed "tongue grafting," reminding readers that "root and scion must be the same size" in order "to make these little trees." Owen Albright, from Leesburg, Florida, opted for the "wedge graft"; N. B. Howard, also from Florida, chose the "cleft graft"; and W. R. Stuart "whip grafted," a process he deemed "very successful." These techniques were carefully explained in great detail, laid out and illustrated in easily accessible language. The wide range of acceptable techniques on display would have assured fearful growers that in pursuing the new science of grafting, they would not be undermining the old art of choice.[6]

Personal agrarian-based testimonies were persuasive for another reason as well. Farmers generally valued the opportunity that agriculture provided to solve unexpected problems with pragmatic and innovative solutions. This point is easily overlooked, as we tend to view farmers as laborers working from the neck down, pushing the plow more than the envelope of ideas. In many ways, though, they defined themselves as farmers through their own rugged brand of situational ingenuity. Nineteenth-century farmers were by temperament experimenters and communicators. They were tinkerers. They knew better than anyone—certainly better than scientists or tree experts—that nature was fickle and that tampering with it to grow food necessarily had some degree of unpredictability, if not an explicit possibility for fantastic failure. Confronting that unpredictability was, when you got down to it, the essential challenge and appeal of farming. It was what imbued daily grunt work with meaning. It was what rewarded creativity and skill. It was therefore highly encouraging for farmers to find in these published testimonies a clear sense that growers had ample opportunities to solve problems with their own ideas when it came to cultivating orchards with improved varieties. Grafting, farmers were assured, was anything but a formulaic or sterile procedure. It was a technique that encouraged and rewarded something we don't give farmers enough credit for having: creativity.

Small, self-fashioned solutions provided by everyday farmers thus delivered big messages to doubtful planters. When one Florida orchardist found, to his dismay, that only 20 percent of his grafted pecans had succeeded, he did some research and came to the conclusion that they "were sucked by the soldier bugs." Rather than cede power to an army of militant and spiny insects, however, the innovative pecan planter was pleased to report, "I have since covered grafts with mosquito netting with success." When J. H. Girardeau discovered that only 350 of the 1,000 splice-grafted trees that he planted had survived the ravages of wood lice, he traced the problem to his decision to fertilize the orchard with cotton seed, a product that he promptly banned from his farm. A planter named Frank White from Live Oak, Florida, ran into trouble when he used grafting wax to cover his cleft grafts. After considerable experimentation, he found that when he covered the wax with cloth his success rate rose 75 percent. He reported this improvement with evident enthusiasm and pride. Again, though these solutions might seem insignificant in the grand scheme of commercial pecan production, they are central to the story. Farmers who were able to watch their contemporaries overcome quotidian problems with grafting became farmers who were more likely to consider the technological transition to pecan improvement themselves.[7]

Eventually, inspiring stories of commercial success percolated into the mainstream media, making it all the more difficult for prospective orchardists to avoid at least contemplating improved techniques and varieties. A 1930 *Texas Monthly* article highlighted the extraordinary accomplishments of several ordinary farmers who decided to pursue advanced methods of pecan improvement. One woman, Emma B. Klingeman, stood out for her accomplishments. The article explained how "with true pioneer spirit," Mrs. Klingeman "beheaded hundreds of large native trees growing on her [New Braunfels] ranch, and budded them." Five years later, her efforts bore an abundance of fruit, earning Klingeman the honor of owning the largest and most productive grove of top-worked pecans in the world. "Her work," exclaimed the *Monthly*, "has revolutionized pecan growing in Texas and other States." To boot, she had become wealthy from the endeavor.[8]

Klingeman's rise to pecan stardom typified what many agricultural publications were attempting to do between 1900 and 1925. They were hoping to show how everyday planters, in this case a woman with no background in growing pecans, were making the leap toward improved varieties and, as a result, experiencing tangible rewards. Central to these narratives was an underlying emphasis on do-it-yourself simplicity and rugged individualism. Anyone, went the message, could make this change. The *Texas Monthly* piece editorialized: "What this woman has done, others can do." As far as formal training went, the article quoted the head of the state's "Nut Division," who explained, "Some people have the idea that a person has to attend some school or work with some expert a year as an apprentice before he can bud a pecan tree." "This," he declared, "is absurd." Indeed, he went on to note that one could learn to be an effective bud grafter over a short afternoon spent with an experienced orchardist or extension agent. No expertise was required, a factor that would have been especially appealing to farmers who lacked formal agricultural education and were averse to becoming dependent on nurserymen for scion and stock.[9]

Judging by the number of pecan orchardists who adopted improved methods of pecan propagation in the opening decades of the twentieth century, it appears that these messages cajoling farmers to do it themselves were not implausible. The USDA took note of the popular transition to improved varieties, which was well under way by 1912. "Comparatively few orchards of grafted trees were planted before 1900," it wrote. However, "since that time . . . the planting of pecan orchards in the Southern States has been taking place at a rapidly accelerating rate." "Most unusual interest," it added, "is being manifested in pecan culture." For this most unusual interest it could thank the efforts of agricultural scientists and other experts who had learned that how they communicated with farmers was just as important as the content that they hoped to communicate. After a quarter century of trying to persuade pecan growers to embrace the virtues of grafting, the USDA and the extension agents that followed its lead finally triumphed in winning over farmers to the cause that Landrum, back in 1822, had, however inadvertently, foreseen as crucial to the future of pecan trees.[10]

The second major reason that farmers came to appreciate and embrace the advice doled out by USDA experts had to do with insects—specifically, the relative success that the USDA had in the national quest to fight insects with insecticides. Although this factor might seem unrelated to the cause of pecans, it is anything but. Between 1870 and 1900 the United States was hit hard with wave after wave of insect attacks on its most precious and valued cash crops. Virtual plagues of locusts, cinch bugs, potato beetles, gypsy moths, and corn borers— among other insidious six-legged invaders—reduced millions of dollars' worth of grain, potatoes, and vegetables to costly piles of agricultural waste. As these pests did their work, desperate farmers looked to anyone capable of offering viable and—even better—immediate solutions. The USDA, armed with chemistry, stepped up to do battle.

These massive insect outbreaks were, in essence, the USDA's first major test of its legitimacy since its inception in 1862. USDA scientists dithered for a while among biological, cultural, and chemical responses. Eventually, however, they put their weight behind the chemical option. "Let us spray!" declared one acolyte of the chemical path. That is precisely what farmers did, with something of a rage. For a solid two decades agents spanned the country and advised farmers to essentially douse their fields with two solutions in particular—Paris green and London purple. Putting aside for now the long-term health consequences of these mixtures (the active agents are arsenic and lead, respectively), and putting aside for now the long-term environmental consequences wrought by the concoctions (both severely damage aquatic ecosystems and human nervous systems), the short-term consequences among early adopters were undeniable: the insecticides, lo and behold, worked.[11]

Paris green and London purple eventually posed such a potent health threat that European importers of American grain and dried fruit declared a boycott on American products until these agents were replaced with safer alternatives. European health concerns mattered little, however, to the nineteenth-century farmers who were seeing these agents salvage their crops, or at least significantly reduce the damage caused to them. This precedent was set just as the grafting question was coming to the fore, and it was an important one for pecan producers to witness. The USDA pushed a new solution, desperate farmers accepted it, and—again, relatively speaking (and speaking in the short term)—the solution was effective. The upshot was a notable boost in reputation for a federal agency that since its inception in 1862 had been looked at askance by farmers accustomed to keeping their own collective council on matters entomological. Surely this qualified success had the side effect of predisposing more pecan growers to at least prick up a curious ear when the outside experts began singing the praises of grafting a crop that had for so long been valued for its status as a low-maintenance fruit. The USDA was no oracle, but as pecan farmers recognized, history showed it could make life much easier for those who tilled the soil for a living. So long as they would listen.

Another beneficial aspect of the USDA's insecticide program—at least when it came to encouraging farmers to accept advanced pecan-growing methods—centered again on the farmer-scientist relationship. The branch of the USDA most directly involved in promoting insecticide sprays was the

Division of Entomology. For whatever reason, the nation's earliest federal entomologists were men who brought to their job considerable agricultural experience. The leading federal entomologists had worked the land. They understood farms, farming, and farmers; they grasped how the agricultural mind worked, and appreciated how farmers could be appealed to and, with any luck, convinced to undertake what were advertised to be beneficial changes. As a result, they established an effective working relationship with average farmers. As we have seen, pecan agents emulated this relationship with considerable success.[12]

The point here might require a little elaboration. Given that we are trying to understand exactly how and why many pecan growers were willing, over a modest twenty-year period, to essentially rethink the basic meaning of the pecan tree, it would seem most logical to focus on the technology itself—grafting—and the benefits that it conveyed. However, again, to focus on the technology alone is to overlook one of the more elusive but important aspects of any sort of technology transfer: the social context in which that shift in knowledge takes place. Agricultural scientists and nurserymen had been promoting the virtues of grafted varieties for many decades before they were accepted en masse by southern orchardists who had previously been wedded to passively cultivated groves and the obvious convenience of seedlings. What eventually pushed most skeptical growers over the technological brink was not the "truth" of grafting's possible effectiveness—that information had been out there for a while. Instead, it was the nature of the context in which they adopted it. It is on this point that entomologists, perhaps more than any other group of scientific experts within the rapidly expanding USDA, proved to be the most diplomatic and effective agents of pecan modernization.

Given their agricultural background, entomologists were very attuned to the often idiosyncratic ways in which farmers pursued agricultural change. Growers preferred to arrive at their own conclusions through a process that one historian has called a "chaos of experimentation." They were, at heart, experts in the game of trial and error. Agricultural entomologists, whose singular goal it was to kill the animals they studied, thus solicited input from farmers at the outset, as it was the farmer alone who could report on the destruction his crops were experiencing. Entomologists hired farmers to collect and, in some cases, analyze data on insect populations and life cycles, and when a critical mass of information had been accumulated, they worked closely with farmers to arrive at a realistic solution. More often than not, this was done with deference to the farmer's on-the-ground authority, which both parties knew was more useful than any sort of laboratory investigation. As a result, the resulting working relationship was in most respects a healthy one, one that ensured that a bond of trust and mutual respect would form between farmers and agricultural authorities with fancy credentials.[13]

Furthermore, entomologists themselves were valuable friends for the pecan orchardist to have. The more pecan farmers moved in the direction of cultivated varieties, the more vulnerable their trees became to insect depredations. As we have seen, one commonly recognized benefit of passively cultivating wild trees, or planting seedlings, was that broad genetic diversity precluded the uniformity that insect species quickly evolved to consume. Pecan groves were commonly (and accurately) seen to be relatively free from insect pest problems, as Bacon himself fully recognized when he wrote, "Of all the valuable food producing trees, the pecan is attacked by fewer insects or fungal diseases than almost any other tree." This was, of course, true only while the trees were in their wild, or passively cultivated, state.[14]

Bacon, for all his love of cultivars, had to admit that "persons who say that the Pecan is entirely free from insect enemies are in error." The pecan nut casebearer, the pecan weevil, the hickory shuck worm, the pecan leaf casebearer, the spittlebug, the fall webworm, and the pecan budmoth were just a few of the insects that were becoming household words for pecan orchardists. The common recommendation was to spray with inorganic pesticides—calcium arsenate, nicotine sulfate, and mineral oil emulsions were common. The problem before the advent of DDT in the 1940s and the concomitant air blast sprayers was the lack of machinery to spray with any sort of effectiveness. Very few pecan orchardists invested in the two-man hydraulic sprayer. Farmers instead often resorted to methods of cultural control, such as planting cowpeas to lure insects away from pecans, or discerning what levels of fertilizer and soil moisture might keep insects at bay. Whatever methods were used, it is important to note that insect infestations were a direct result of farmers' choosing to narrow the genetic variation of the pecans by planting uniform cultivars.[15]

As a result, pecan orchardists would have no choice but to work on some level with entomological experts. That was part of the trade-off when it came to controlling, rather than striking a balance with, nature. The Division of Entomology's impressive track record with respect to both working with farmers and providing effective solutions proved to be pivotal in nudging farmers toward more standardized and improved practices in the fertile opening decades of the twentieth century.[16]

If these two social factors were critical in perpetuating the onset of improved pecan varieties, another, much more tangible factor also played an influential role in making the years from 1900 to 1925 such an important transitional period for the pecan tree. This was the recognition that improved varieties of pecans could, if properly adopted, profitably move into many southern locations where pecans rarely, if ever, grew naturally. They could, as we have seen, make appearances in non-native locales. With cotton crops increasingly suffering attacks from the boll weevil, pecans began to have more appeal as an alternative crop in inland areas, as well as in places such as California, Florida, and South Carolina. This expansion into virgin territory was the simplest and probably the most critical prerequisite for substantial long-term change, the kind that would make places like Georgia and New Mexico global centers of pecan production. Through this potential, the recognition gradually emerged that as the pecan industry took off, pecans that were uniform and of consistent high quality could make the orchardist a decent living, if not more than that. "Money," declared one popular magazine article on the pecan, "really does grow on trees."[17]

The one pest that had defied the efforts of extension agents to achieve clear results with insecticides was the boll weevil. The weevil entered Texas in 1892 from Mexico, and by the early 1900s it had achieved a notorious status as one of the most devastating pests that ever entered the United States. This insect was so voracious in its quest to destroy cotton, and exacted so much actual damage, that it encouraged many southern growers to switch their horticultural efforts to pecans.[18] Growing pecans away from riverbanks, however, was best done with the improved varieties. The chief of the Texas Department of Agriculture was the first to advocate this transition, explaining, "If a farmer spends only two or three days labor on a pecan tree, that tree will make more clear profit than an acre of cotton per year." He added, "The cotton . . . requires as much time each year as it would take to complete a new top on a pecan tree." *Texas Monthly* echoed that advice, calling the improved pecan "a potentially great product that may shove King Cotton from his throne." Even from the scholarly trenches, a Texas A&M professor opined in 1922 that "the time is probably not very remote when the South will boast as loudly of her pecan industry as she now does her cotton." Cultivars made this kind of thinking possible.[19]

This was heady promotional talk, of course. However, the science of pecan improvement lent it some ballast. Enough pecan growers had, throughout the nineteenth century, passively cultivated enough wild inland varieties that there was plenty of established inland stock for farmers to improve upon. The great benefit of working with these preexisting trees was that they had developed the "hardiness" required to both survive and produce fruit under drier conditions. As the grafting pioneer E. E. Risien wrote in 1909, "In our western and southwestern pecans we see so many varieties improve by mere chance that there certainly is reason to believe that the reward must someday be great to the pecan breeder." The plan to "preserve and intensify the desirable qualities of those [pecan trees] we already have" ensured that improvements would be consistent with the vagaries of geographical reality. For example, the pecan trees already adapted to this environment shared the quality of maintaining their enormously long taproots. Pecan trees growing closer to riverbanks relied more on lateral roots and, as a result, allowed their taproots to eventually rot and fall off. It was through the improvement of these well-adapted inland varieties that one grower could remark, without exaggeration, that "the finest and most productive trees I have seen have been raised on well drained upland."[20]

The proliferation of the boll weevil also helps explain why, between 1900 and 1920, Georgia temporarily edged out Texas as the emerging center of commercial pecan production. As we have seen, production rose in Georgia from 30,000 to more than 2 million pounds of pecans in just over two decades. With the advent of commercial varieties it became common for northern land development companies to purchase large tracts of land in Georgia and Florida and rent the land to growers. When more planters in Georgia decided to grow pecans instead of cotton they had no choice but to commit themselves to higher-yielding, improved varieties. The risk would have been too high otherwise. Pecans, after all, didn't grow wild in Georgia, and we have seen what happened when farmers held to the idea of growing from seed. Nurserymen and breeders thus worked incessantly to make improvements consistent with the soil quality and climate of central and southern Georgia. In Texas, by contrast, orchardists could drag their feet a bit, mainly because the abundance of wild specimens allowed them to do so. The *McIntosh County Democrat* chastised state pecan growers in 1927: "The farmers of this county have overlooked their best bet when they failed to put our improved pecans on their land or to have the mature trees budded."[21]

Indeed, in Texas this process of domestication evolved more slowly. The desire to improve varieties was always somewhat hampered by the fact that the state was generously endowed with so many wild pecan trees—about 80 million in 1926. So as the pecan became more attractive in light of the cotton boll weevil outbreak, there was always a built-in incentive to exploit preexisting wild groves and, yet again, rely on passive cultivation. As *Texas Monthly* reported, "the vast majority of these eighty million trees are growing in the wilderness, crowded out by other timber and sapped by undergrowth. Millions of them never bear a pecan." (This was not quite the case, as many of the trees bore heavy crops, despite being barren most years. The comment is more a reflection of how nature's cycles did not conform to man's economic cycles.) If Texas farmers did anything in terms of improvement during the first decades of the twentieth century, they would top-work trees. As one report noted, "Farmers are drawing dividends on papershell pecans that were [top] budded a few years ago to better varieties." With Georgia leaping ahead in the game of pecan improvement by bringing millions of improved varieties to land that never supported a wild pecan, Texans, according to the *Monthly*, were justified in doing only one thing: "We should hang our heads in shame about it."[22]

Not so in other regions. Georgia may have been the leader in the transition to cultivated pecans, but other areas of the United States soon capitalized on improved varieties as well. By 1920, the *Los Angeles Times* was able to report that "there seems to be little question but that good budded pecan trees, grown in the right localities in Southern California, will produce, with an ample supply of water, crops as great as the average in Texas." A nursery in Riverside, as it turned out, was already marketing a local cultivar called the Crane, and it was said to be "bearing heavy crops of excellent pecans." Arizona became engaged in pecan production as well. After testing 350 varieties of pecan, experimental planters concluded that five cultivars—Halbert, Kincaid, Burkett, Sovereign, and Success—readily adapted to high-desert conditions. By 1925 the state was putting about 15,000 pecan trees into the ground a year—not a huge number, but a start. South Carolina, too, jumped in alongside Georgia. By 1932 it was exporting pecans throughout the United States, especially to New York City, perhaps as a result of the heavy investment in southeastern orchards coming from New York.[23]

If the potential for geographical expansion during the reign of the boll weevil aided the popularity of cultivars, the ultimate appeal in cultivating improved varieties came down to the simple fact that they were proving to be quite profitable as a stand-alone cash crop. This perspective was, by the 1920s, a novel one. Even as late as the early twentieth century, close observers of the pecan trade continued to view the business as something of an economic and agricultural sideshow. Harold Hume, writing in 1906, noted the "many orchards of considerable size, planted with meritorious budded and grafted varieties," but he also noted how "the product of these plantings is entirely used by what may be termed a private trade, either by seedsmen or by private individuals for dessert purposes." The "export trade," he added, was "comparatively undeveloped." In other words, in 1906 and well beyond, pecan farming was still considered a niche endeavor. Others viewed pecan keeping as an addendum to more-mainstream work, profitable as a backup in difficult times but hardly worthy of a primary economic quest. Bacon, in 1902, advised potential growers to think about their pecan groves as they might a life insurance policy.[24]

It was again during these pivotal two decades, however, that this opinion began to change, at least with some growers. A pecan planter from Coleman, Texas, laid out the economic logic of taking the pecan to the level of a cash crop, or, as we've seen others suggest, to the exalted status of cotton:

> *There is a vast difference in the quality of the wild and improved pecan nuts and a consequent difference in prices. The wild varieties bring from 3 to 6 cents per pound; not much more than good wages for gathering; while the improved varieties bring at wholesale from 20 to 50 cents per pound, and some of the fancy kind, for planting purposes, from $1 to $3 per pound. Making a conservative estimate of 20 trees per acre, with an average of 50 pounds per tree, the wild nuts at 4 cents are worth $40 per acre, whereas the superior varieties at 20 cents will bring $200 per acre.*[25]

Whereas few farmers were capitalizing upon this economic logic in 1904 (when the planter did his math), thousands of them were doing so by the early 1920s. Indeed, the nature of the industry, as well as the market it served, had changed significantly. Consider the 1928 assessment of J. D. Pope, an agricultural economist with the Alabama Extension Service. "You have seen this industry develop," he wrote, "from the relatively low valued product of wild and seedlings trees to a six to nine billion dollar business, a substantial part of which value consists of a product of excellent quality which is growing in favor with the consuming public." Taking a bird's-eye view of this emerging industry, it stood to reason that economic prospects were ripe for pecan growers who were willing to embrace cultivated trees. The pecan's "comparatively restricted planting area," as the *Los Angeles Times* put it, not only "argues against the dangers of overproduction," but it ensured to growers huddled in this "planting area" sole access to a "world wide market." Growers were nowhere near achieving such scope, but the goal was being articulated and envisioned for those willing to follow it.[26]

One trend reflecting the changed nature of the pecan business—the elevation of pecan cultivation to a primary endeavor—was one of the more popular varietals planted in states that had not, before the emergence of improved cultivars, harbored wild pecans. The varietal was called, aptly enough, "the Moneymaker." Indeed, an enterprising farmer could dedicate his career to cultivating this crop. The primary reason for this opportunity was the emergence and popular embrace of improved varieties. Thus did biological knowledge, the social politics of expertise, and the profit motive combine to challenge the fundamental nature of America's native nut.[27]

CHAPTER 6

"Pecans for the World"

THE PECAN GOES INDUSTRIAL,
1920–1945

If scientific agriculture came of age in the late 1800s, modern agribusiness arose in full force after World War I. Between 1920 and 1945, American farming matured into a substantial industry led by growers who built large plantations and relentlessly produced only a single crop. A potent combination of forces—technical, political, and ideological—converged to transform agriculture in the United States from a regional-based, diverse endeavor into the most productive, economically rationalized, and mono-cropping agricultural system the world had ever seen. Hybrid seeds, tractors, mechanized plows, nitrogen fertilizer, refrigerated cars, pesticide blasters, and scores of other transformative innovations not only enabled fewer farmers to feed more people but elevated the U.S. to the status of the world's undisputed breadbasket. When we evaluate this historical development, we tend to focus on corn, wheat, beef, pork, and other dominant staple commodities. A host of less-explored food products, however, decisively rode the wave of this revolution as well, and some of them—such as the pecan—managed to stake out geographical ground so well matched to its growth potential, so finely tuned to its biological needs, that orchardists were able to reach untapped markets by the end of World War II.[1]

None of this productive ingenuity came easy. As William Henry Chandler, the author of the 1928 book *North American Orchards*, explained, the transition from passive to active cultivation in the pecan industry was not a decision to be taken lightly. "The cost of the budded trees, the use of expensive land or the laborious and expensive cultivation of cheap hill land, the controlling of diseases and insects, and the maintenance of soil fertility," he wrote, "make the growing of pecan orchards a very different enterprise from merely finding productive old wild trees that have survived the competition and the adversaries on unused land." Building and maintaining a commercial orchard, in essence, was a fundamentally different endeavor, one that demanded not the peripheral interest of an agricultural hobbyist but the exclusive focus of a full-time orchardist. Not all planters were willing to make the leap. Enough were, however, to industrialize the pecan.[2]

*Commercial pecan farming—as opposed to supplemental pecan farming—*had a steep learning curve. As the social, economic, and environmental factors described in the last chapter eventually persuaded many pioneering pecan growers to embrace the inherent logic of pecan improvement, they found themselves facing a daunting array of novel challenges. Having made the leap toward improvement, they now had to master its techniques, adhere to its rhythms, and find new markets. In the era of pecan improvement, every pecan grower encountered dozens of unfamiliar questions and situations. This was especially true before the 1930s, when affordable and specialized nurseries became the norm. The first commercial pecan growers to use improved varieties would often have no choice but to improve them on their own. Which was fine with them.

This was also a time when general knowledge about the basics of cultivating pecan orchards with improved varieties became accessible and increasingly standardized. Farmers would always harbor a certain amount of suspicion and maintain decision-making leeway when it came to growing pecans, but as orchards of improved varieties overtook passive cultivation and seedlings between 1920 and 1940, a set of basic practices came to dominate the production of commercial pecans from California to South Carolina. There was, of course, no such thing as a "typical pecan farmer," but most commercial pecan orchards followed a general set of agricultural practices and processes. With the implementation of these increasingly uniform practices and processes, national pecan production gradually matured into a profitable, standardized, and industrialized branch of American agribusiness, routinely producing bumper crops of improved pecan nuts alongside the wild specimens that never left the market.

As pecan farmers slowly adopted grafted varieties, an extensive literature emerged to assist their efforts. At the turn of the century it was especially common for growers to abandon seedling orchards altogether and attempt to graft their own stock on their own terms—an option that was, as we saw in the last chapter, extremely important to them. For the first decade of the twentieth century, most pecan farmers served as their own inexpert, ad hoc nurserymen. While there were dozens of ways to graft, one homegrown, relatively accessible method came to dominate: a process called "patch budding." The "patch bud"—first popularized in the 1910s—became an easy and widely embraced alternative to the labor-intensive process of climbing into and top-working pecan trees. Rather than removing the tree's top and awaiting new growth into which a fresh bud could be inserted, a patch bud could be easily inserted into the lower bark of a young tree's trunk, or even into one of the tree's larger limbs. Farmers undertook this project in the early spring when the bark would still "slip," thus allowing for its easy removal and the bud's secure insertion. As for the budwood itself, pecan growers cut "strong, vigorous shoots"—about eight to twenty inches—from desirable trees, bundled them, and packed the bundle in sand, sawdust, or sphagnum moss until samples were needed. Great care had to be taken to keep these buds dormant until it was time for patching them, early in the spring. A sprouting bud, after all, wasn't even good enough for cheap kindling, as it was too moist to burn.

The rule of thumb was that a patch bud should be set in young seedling trees whose trunks had yet to grow beyond six to eight inches in diameter. Farmers set the patch in a section of the tree located about four inches above the ground, either in the trunk or in an upward portion of a limb close to the trunk. Preparing the spot for the insertion of a bud graft took some finesse. First the bark had to be shaved down with a paring knife to equal lengths on both bud and stock. Then, with a budding knife (the most popular brand being the "Texas Aggie budding knife"), farmers made two identical parallel incisions about an inch apart on both the stock and the bud, followed by vertical slits about half an inch apart. The resulting square patch of bark was, like a Band-Aid, gently peeled from the stock, creating space for the bud, which was then delicately patched in. One square of bark replaced another. "The bud," wrote one popular manual, "should fit snugly into its new location."[3]

Once inserted—one manual advised to "make the transfer rapidly so as to prevent the drying out of the exposed cellular tissues"—the bud was tied down with thin string and covered with grafting wax. When the wax dried, farmers removed the string and then "forced" the bud—in essence, snipped the top of the sapling and removed competing native buds, thereby channeling nutrients into the designated graft and stimulating the release of hormones that sparked dormant buds on the graft to come alive. When the selected bud began to grow, they staked it and carefully monitored its progress.[4] Other methods of bud grafting were certainly popular—chip grafting, bark grafting, whip grafting, ring budding. But the patch bud was a staple procedure upon which the pecan industry—patch by patch, graft by graft, orchard by orchard—traveled on the journey from wild to cultivated. To be sure, many forms of grafting were employed by many pecan farmers, but the patch bud was the most accessible and arguably the most common method of do-it-yourself improvement.

Properly locating an orchard was just as important as the ability to bud and graft trees effectively. While improved varieties allowed growers to plant on both upland and bottomland plots, it remained critical to the long-term health of an orchard that farmers chose areas with especially rich and deep soil. The pecan is an unusually deep-rooted and long-lived tree. As a result, orchardists were duly advised to choose land with soil that would enable the trees to draw nourishment for "perhaps eighty to a hundred years." Assessing such a rate of fertility, farmers sought soil with a proven record of producing thirty to forty bushels of corn or one half to a full bale of cotton per acre. Another way to help ensure that soil had proper fertility for pecan production was to prepare the land by planting a season or two of a staple crop followed by a layer of green manure (rotting plant debris). After breaking the soil, churning in the manure, and waiting a month, the grower could plant the grafted saplings with a greater measure of confidence. This initial planting usually took place between December 1 and February 15.[5]

Setting the trees could never be done in a haphazard manner. Growers with commercial ambitions typically sought to plant on at least ten cleared acres. On such a plot orchardists could expect to plant anywhere from 200 to 230 trees. The key was to place the trees close enough to maximize density but far enough apart to allow room for ample canopy expansion. A fifty-to-sixty-foot distance was considered normal. Should one err, though, he was advised to err on the side of offering trees too much room for growth. As one grower explained, "For ultimate, maximum results, trees must have distance, and plenty of it."[6] Some orchardists planted densely and then culled the weaker specimens as they emerged. A leading manual of the day, however, disagreed with this approach, explaining, "It is better economy to allow the desired distance and then utilize the unused space with annual crops until the trees need all the room." Either way, farmers had to space trees uniformly.[7]

Planting grafted trees could be physically harder than one might expect. Holes had to be dug several feet deep, usually with a post auger, because pecan saplings have unusually long taproots (in some cases, the taproot of a mature pecan can be longer than the trunk). Some farmers dug shallow holes, snipped off the taproot, and planted. For this literal shortcut, though, they often paid dearly, as such trees would subsequently not produce as well. "The tap root can be cut back to within twenty or twenty-four inches without serious damage," explained the authors of *Pecan Growing*, "but better results are usually secured by leaving the entire root system, except the bruised and broken parts." Planters were urged to keep sapling roots moist during the transfer by wrapping them in wet towels or carrying young trees to the orchard in barrels of water. Once the sapling had been planted, the topsoil had to be tightly secured around all the roots to prevent air pockets from forming and drying them out. This stage of the process was both exceedingly labor-intensive and demanding of a certain amount of finesse.[8]

After the saplings had been successfully grafted and entered into a gridded plot, what many considered to be the real work began—defending the trees from all kinds of external dangers. Young pecan trees remained vulnerable to a variety of threats, all of which orchardists had to diligently manage. We have already heard about the insect menace. Other common problems also included "sun scald," a condition that afflicted trees when the canopy had not yet filled to the point that it could shade the tree trunk. There were also rodents, which, attracted to the soft bark, could easily girdle a sapling and kill it. To deal with these threats after planting saplings, farmers were advised to cover their tree trunks with newspaper. They also pruned the tops in order to keep the trees relatively low to the ground and to make it easier to spray more uniformly. Overall, these threats, which could easily undermine an entire orchard, and thus an entire investment, never waned. They warranted constant vigilance and should remind us how difficult life was for people who grew food. Such was life when working with a handful of pecan varieties rather than copses in which every tree has its own genetic identity.

Adding to the burden of these myriad tasks was the fact that the pecan payoff was anything but immediate. Pecans took longer to reach maturity than any other orchard tree. An orchard of improved pecans might start producing token yields after a few years, but it typically took at least eight years for trees to begin masting at full throttle and as many as fifteen years before they reached peak production. As a result of this frustrating delay, some pecan farmers diversified their nascent pecan orchards with a variety of complementary crops. Herein lay room for ample creativity (although it is a creativity that today no orchardist would remotely tolerate).

One of the most popular inter-cropping schemes came out of Texas A&M University. Agricultural scientists there had good luck planting a crop of Irish potatoes, followed immediately by a planting of sweet potatoes. "As a result of the constant stirring of soil and unused fertilizer," explained one report, "the young trees make excellent growth under this plan." Other farmers had notable success with crops of eggplant, tomatoes, velvet beans, soybeans, peanuts, and peppers. After harvest, the green manure could be churned back into the soil with a plow. A California grower commented that "pecan trees, with their long, deep tap roots, are relatively independent of intercrops." One farmer was a vocal advocate of "plant[ing] his orchard to pasture and keep[ing] a herd of sheep grazing on the land." Complementary crops, and animals, almost always worked well, so long as pecan orchardists kept in mind that "the young pecan trees are to be given the right of way over all other crops grown on the same land."[9]

Equally critical to the pecan industry's rise to the vaunted power of national producer was the ongoing, and increasingly refined, process of matching developed pecan varieties to particular geographical regions and conditions. This initially decentralized and often haphazard process was ultimately rationalized by the rise of commercial nurseries, relevant USDA agencies, and a variety of state pecan growers' associations, all of which came of age during this period. The emergence of these institutions, however, was ultimately dependent on the work of hundreds of lone pecan pioneers—men working in the fields, experimenting, experimenting some more, and building, through trial and error, on the success of Antoine's graft to decide which varieties worked best in which locations.

It is impossible to say how many cultivars were developed, grown, and then abandoned in the late nineteenth and early twentieth centuries. Theoretically, since every tree reproduced from seed is genetically unique, billions would have been possible. We do know, though, that pecan farmers were constantly tinkering with new stock and that, over time, a few breeders were able to lay claim to cultivars that had staying power. These were named and tracked into the future. One year before the Centennial pecan made its debut at the Centennial Exposition in Philadelphia, a retired New Orleans cotton trader and horticulture enthusiast named Colonel W. R. Stuart bought a plot of land in Ocean Springs, Mississippi, and began experimenting systematically with pecan grafting. The fruits of his labor were unusually abundant.

Starting with a hundred seedlings obtained from Mobile and New Orleans, Stuart developed several cultivars so hardy and productive that they continue to be planted widely to this day. These varieties include the Russell, the Pabst, and, most appropriately, the Stuart, which constitutes a quarter of all contemporary orchard trees. The Stuart's popularity derives primarily from its high yields, large nut size, and relatively impressive resistance to disease.[10]

Other pecan entrepreneurs quickly followed. One of Colonel Stuart's employees at Ocean Springs was Theodore Bechtel. A clear natural when it came to developing hearty cultivars, Bechtel, who began working for Stuart in 1899, soon purchased land and started a small nursery of his own. From it emerged the Success in 1903 and soon thereafter the Candy, a variety designed for use by confectionaries. In Texas, an English immigrant named Edmond E. Risien began propagating pecans at the confluence of the San Saba and Colorado Rivers. Risien experimented with thousands of nuts taken from a single tree located on the east bank of the San Saba. He went on to be called the "Johnny Appleseed of pecans." His goal was to develop varieties conducive to drier, western climates. "He was sold on pecans," his great-granddaughter later explained, "and he wanted everyone to be sold on them." From his efforts emerged the San Saba, San Saba Improved, Onliwon, Texas Prolific, and Western. All these varieties made the expansion of commercial pecan orchards into west Texas, New Mexico, Arizona, and California a viable commercial possibility. Risien eventually established his own profitable nursery as well.[11]

Many Texan growers followed in Risien's footsteps to pioneer varieties that became best sellers among orchardists ranging from California to Florida. In Coleman, Texas, Herbert Halbert developed the self-styled Halbert, a variety that—when crossed with a Mahan cultivar—led to the Wichita, which constitutes 10 percent of today's pecan market (because it is prone to pecan scab in humid environments, it's mostly grown west of the Balcones Escarpment). Halbert himself was an aggressive top-budder—mainly because his land flooded so often. Sadly, he died at the age of seventy-eight after falling from high up in a pecan tree. In Burnet County, Texas, J. H. Burkett helped to push the pecan industry even farther west with the development of drought-tolerant cultivars, most notably the Burkett, a variety so successful that it earned Burkett, armed with his third-grade education, a position as head of Texas's Division of Edible Nuts. This office, the only one of its kind in the world, became a fertile spot of ingenuity, with breeders acquiring experimental land in Brownwood, Texas, and pioneering dozens of new varieties. One identifying feature of the Brownwood cultivars is that they were almost all named after Native American groups, including the Caddo, the Mohawk, the Apache, the Cheyenne, the Cherokee, the Pawnee, the Sioux, and the Wichita. Each variety remains popular to this day.[12]

In time, however, pecan growers were experiencing too much of a good thing. There is no doubt that in many cases improved varieties were living up to their potential. In some respects, though, the chaos of experimentation led more to chaos than experimentation. By the 1920s, many orchardists decided that a surplus of varieties was on the market and that most of them were of mediocre quality at best and not worth tracking. So saturated was the market in a clutter of cultivars that the National Pecan Growers Association, declaring that "a confusing number of varieties was being grown," developed a task force to categorize the 620 known varieties in existence into the following designations: "standard," "promising," "on trial," "doubtful," "unworthy," and "unpropagated." In the end, 31 of those varieties were deemed standard. Another 66 were categorized as promising. This rating would narrow the planters' options considerably, which most planters considered to be a good thing.[13]

Of equal, and related, importance was the fact that the National Pecan Growers Association made significant progress in dividing pecan growers into eleven geographical regions and matching relevant varieties to those eleven landscape types. This effort proved to be invaluable, especially for new planters entering the industry who were unfamiliar with the range of available cultivars. To cite just a few examples, growers in southern Oklahoma and Arkansas were advised to adopt the Alley, Burkett, Moneymaker, Stuart, Success, Schley, and Pabst. Orchardists in Arizona, New Mexico, and California were directed to the San Saba, Western, Onliwon, Halbert, and Kincaid. Central and northeast Texas favored the Bradley, Burkett, Curtis, Stuart, San Saba Improved, Western, and the (regrettably named) Boggus. Varieties dismissed as "doubtful" included the Zink, Pearl, Forester, and Stringfellow. Those that were still unpropagated, and thus untested, included the San Marcos, Lady Finger, Kidney, and, in a depressing sign of the Jim Crow times, the Nigger. C. A. Reed, a USDA pomologist, reminded pecan farmers that "not a single variety now known is without its drawbacks." At the same time, he told them that it would not be long before "the question of varieties [would] be settled." It was an ongoing process, one that continues to this day as pecan orchardists seek the best varieties for the often changing conditions of agricultural life.[14]

As the developing and slowly consolidating industry cohered around increasingly standardized planting practices and cultivars, and as nurserymen and farmers began to match pecan varieties with specific geographical conditions (however imperfectly), pecan trees were becoming carefully managed commodities rather than natural aspects of the southern landscape. The wild was being cultivated and rationalized, the chaos of experimentation was yielding to a semblance of order, and the pecan industry was cohering into something unified and potentially global in scope. As this transition took place, farmers began to accomplish something both indicative of American agribusiness as a whole and suggestive of its profitable future: they began to churn out higher yields. Matching different varieties to different climates ensured some level of predictability with respect to how much a tree could produce and what an external market might receive. This ability to project an estimated yield was something that passive cultivation never allowed, but it should not be overstated. Because of the pecan's inconsistent bearing schedule, boom and bust cycles can overwhelm collective increases in production. Still, more-predictable yields—even if only slightly more predictable—allowed farmers to think about pecans much as they did other staple crops. Greater predictability also enabled them to think about their product in strictly commercial terms. By the 1930s there were full-fledged pecan farmers doing little else than growing as many pecans as they could coax the land to yield.

Yield increases could reach dramatic numbers once a tree survived the infant stage. The numbers, while perpetually inconsistent as a result of the pecan's alternate masting schedule, were nevertheless, on balance, impressive. A planter who set out an orchard of San Sabas in 1908 would have seen an average yield of 5.52 pounds per tree in 1915, 17.95 in 1918, and a whopping 47 pounds in 1921. A planter who chose Frotschers in 1908 would have seen average tree yields go from 5.9 pounds in 1918, to 34.5 pounds in 1918, to 63.35 pounds in 1921. As for a Moneymaker planted in 1908, it could be expected to yield 11.23 pounds in 1915, 33.92 pounds in 1918, and 52 pounds in 1921. Once mature, these trees could live into old age—80 years or so—and continue to produce 50-plus pounds at least once every three years. It was thought that if one had enough land to stagger production—because masting did not occur annually—he could build a viable business on the back of these figures. In fact, for reasons that are poorly understood, trees planted in even and odd years would eventually fall into a synchronous bearing pattern.[15]

For all the fluctuations in yield figures, by the end of the 1930s southern pecan farmers had formed themselves into a loosely organized industry capable of producing enough pecans to collectively and consistently reach national markets. No crop, however, rises to an industrial scale on the basis of productive cultivars and relatively standardized practices alone. Ushering the industry into larger markets was a broader network of supporting factors. Three of them stand out: (a) the pecan industry began to benefit from federal policies; (b) the industry began to aggressively market itself to potential consumers, many of whom were unfamiliar with the subtle pleasures of the pecan; and (c) shelling machines emerged to keep up with burgeoning rates of production.

The 1930s were a time of unusually active federal involvement in the economy of the United States as a whole. Nowhere was this participation more significant than in the agricultural sector. Corn and other cash crops accounted for the bulk of federal largesse as price supports, protective tariffs, and subsidies cushioned the agricultural economy from inevitable declines. Pecans came in for their share of help as well. In 1937 the Agricultural Adjustment Administration, after intense lobbying by the Pecan Stabilization Association, designed a program intended to assist the export of both shelled and unshelled pecans. The goal of this program, according to the *New York Times*, was "to aid the industry to establish permanent foreign markets." Basically, if a pecan farmer could ship a minimum of 2,000 pounds of pecans, the government guaranteed him a payment of 12 cents per pound. In 1938, the Federal Surplus Commodities Corporation spent $54 million to purchase crop surpluses, part of which went to buy 3.6 million pounds of pecans. By 1942, the Commodity Credit

Corporation was providing low-interest and easily acquired loans to the American Pecan Growers Association. These programs foreshadowed others to come. For now, the fact that the government "insured a market for everything that farmers could produce" was a boon to the pecan industry at the very moment when pecans were on the cusp of becoming an industrialized product. To a very significant extent, the pecan industry became an industry by virtue of the generosity of federal support.[16]

A related factor underscoring the industrialization of pecan production involved direct-marketing efforts. As late as 1926, a USDA official could accurately explain how "pecans are among many of the high class food products grown in the United States which have not yet become essential in the food supply of the world." Both private trade associations and state departments of agriculture worked hard to shift this perception. Motivation for doing so was strong. As indicated, pecan growers were in an enviable position: they were limited to a relatively narrow growing range, had access to improved varieties that were consistently producing high-quality nuts, and were looking into the face of a global market that was completely untapped. As one report noted, "The possibility of building up an export market is almost unlimited," adding, "pecans are grown commercially almost nowhere else in the world outside the United States." The California Department of Agriculture began to promote the pecan as a "distinctively American nut" in an appeal to nationalistic consumption. In 1930, the Federal Farm Board approved the formation of the National Pecan Marketing Association, a commodity cooperative that worked as a merchandising agency. The association's seventeen local cooperative units were expected "to operate through the central agency for the stabilizing of pecan prices." This was something quite necessary, given the "increased output in recent years of about 2000 percent."[17]

The final factor contributing to the industrialization of

pecans centered on the emergence of large-scale shelling machines. Before the rise of mechanical shellers, commercial pecans were sent to large cities such as San Antonio and New Orleans to be shelled by hand—mostly by Mexican immigrants—in hundreds of small shelling plants. By 1930, San Antonio—the undisputed center of pecan shelling—boasted more than four hundred shelling plants. Even small cities supported a few modest shelling operations of their own. Okmulgee, Oklahoma, for example, had four in 1925. Matters changed abruptly and somewhat dramatically, however, in 1938. That was the year that FDR's administration set the wage of pecan shellers at 25 cents an hour. The pecan industry—led by the mammoth Southern Pecan Shelling Company—erupted in protest. It claimed that any wage over 15 cents an hour would cripple the processing business. The company did everything in its power to find loopholes to avoid paying workers the 25-cent wage, including classifying shellers as "learners," a designation that allowed a lower-than-mandated wage. None of the tactics worked. Matters came to a head in October 1938 when the pecan shellers shut their doors and left 50,000 angry workers milling about in the streets of San Antonio.

The fight that dragged on between management and employees proved to be intense.[18] The upshot, however, was all too familiar in the annals of labor history. The dismissal of human workers opened the door for a development that would eventually make human shellers obsolete while allowing the shelling industry to consolidate: mechanical shellers. Mechanical shellers led the way to a highly concentrated industry that could shell and sell as many nuts as planters could grow. By the 1950s, hundreds of shellers had been reduced to about eighty, and about eight of the eighty—located in Chicago, Pittsburgh, and St. Louis—bought almost half of all pecans produced annually.

A typical shelling plant processed millions of pounds of

nuts a year. First they were fed into a large cylindrical drum and spun to clean out dirt and debris. Next, the nuts were fed into a grading machine with ten slots for ten different size categories (most shelling machines used private grades, although federal grades were available). After the nuts were sorted, they were sterilized to "reduce the bacteria and E. Coli count usually present in newly harvested pecans." The nuts were then "soaked in vats of or tanks of chlorinated water" to soften the shell, making it easier to crack and remove. From there they went into giant hoppers, which guided them on conveyor belts into the cracking machines, after which the meat was separated from the shells, and sent to the respective market destinations.[19]

It was a long journey from the grafted variety growing on a pecan plantation in Georgia, Texas, or Louisiana to the conveyor belt of a shelling plant in Pittsburgh, St. Louis, or Chicago. And even after the pecans were cracked, sorted, and bagged, the journey was still not complete. Pecans now had to make their way to American consumers, and American consumers had to eat them. As we shall see, the consumers were more than ready to do their part.

Chapter 7

"In Almost Any Recipe ... Pecans May Be Used"

American Consumers Embrace the Pecan, 1940–1960

The methods and advancements described in the last two chapters consolidated and industrialized pecan production. This development, in turn, resulted in a consistent abundance of domestic pecans. Comments on the crop's explosive production appeared repeatedly in midcentury agricultural discussions. In 1942, the *New York Times* noted that there was a "bumper crop" of pecans. By 1947, the Department of Agriculture reported that "there are 13,000 tons more pecans than in 1946." Georgia alone increased production from 27.5 million pounds to 42 million pounds between those two years. In 1948, the *Times* referred to "this year's record pecan crop," adding, "162,722,000 pounds of pecans are being harvested this fall." The following year brought the same news, with the *Times* referring to "this year's nut harvest, the largest ever to be harvested in the country." Consistent with the upward trend, the year 1951 saw "the second largest crop on record." Reforms initiated to promote pecan production had clearly established an industry whose collective mission was to produce greater amounts of pecans every year. Throughout the 1940s and 1950s, the industry accomplished this task with remarkable regularity, leaving in its wake a vast heap of pecans.[1]

Without an export market for pecans, something had to be

done with them at home. Production increases were worthless without corresponding domestic demand. Pecan producers could rationalize the process of growing choice varieties of nuts until they approached the ultimate apex of modern efficiency, but it meant nothing if American consumers did not do their part. Bottom line: Americans had to buy and eat pecans. Unfortunately for producers, such an expectation could not be taken for granted. Unlike sugar, wheat, or corn, pecans were not a standard feedstock for a variety of processed foods. There were as yet no large industrial buyers ready to gobble up loads of pecans to be used in that way. Throughout the history of the pecan up to this point, consumers had primarily cracked and eaten the nut as a rich and healthy snack during holiday seasons. Additionally, because they were generally more expensive than other nuts, pecans were long considered "the aristocrat among nuts," best reserved for special occasions. It was a reputation that would prove hard to shake, one that persistently kept pecans from reaching their potential as an industrial food product.

With supply as high as it was, producers would have to rely on the culinary creativity of American cooks and consumers to persuade Americans to eat pecans as a staple product. With the benefit of considerable federal involvement, American consumers rose to the challenge, turning pecans from a relative rarity eaten mainly out of the hand during holidays into a common household snack found in everything from salads to soufflés to butter to biscuits to sweet potatoes and, of course, to pralines and pies. Pecans, wrote one industry observer, will "have to be absorbed on the home front." To a remarkable degree, that is exactly what happened. Called upon to eat pecans, Americans obliged. They ate pecans.[2]

The popularization of pecans occurred through a series of discrete developments. The first involved the federal government. It is difficult to overstate precisely how critical the USDA's role was in promoting the pecan as an ideal wartime replacement for meat, much of which was reserved for men in uniform who were doing their part overseas. The agency aggressively spread the message that in an era of food rationing, "nuts, be it remembered in these meat-short days, are a good source of protein." Jane Nickerson, food writer at the *New York Times*, reminded her vast readership in 1945 that "with the scarcity of shortenings in mind, the Government is pointing out that most nuts are at least half fat, and may be used in cooking to impart richness." The *Chicago Daily Tribune* followed suit, promoting the "pecan loaf" as a "good meatless entree for a Friday meal." The government even went so far as to suggest recipes for housewives (and yes, it specified housewives) to undertake. "Home economists," according to one report, "suggest roasting nuts in a little fat in a frying pan, allowing two teaspoons of cooking oil or melted vegetable or table fat and one teaspoon of salt to each cup of nut meats." In 1942, a USDA program deemed pecans "a Victory Food Special." And in 1948, the USDA placed pecans on its hit list of "plentiful foods," thereby encouraging Americans to consume them as an expression of postwar national pride.[3] With federal assistance, the war was good to the pecan.

The government complemented its soft promotion of pecans with harder economic measures. In 1943, to encourage more active consumption by average citizens, it established a price ceiling on pecans and other nuts. The Office of Price Administration aimed to save consumers "at least 10 cents a pound." This measure, not surprisingly, led to a minor insurgency from pecan orchardists, who declared declining prices "a major headache" that was "extremely depressing to growers." The government responded to this discontent in the early 1950s by buying up surplus pecans. In 1952 it scooped into federal coffers more than 3 million pounds of nuts. Flooded every year with an excess of pecans, the government turned around and dumped them on grammar schools throughout the country, where the pecans were fed to captive children held hostage by their school lunch menu. This program worked, but only to a point. One school superintendent from the Chicago area complained that the burden of feeding 800 pounds of pecans to 1,300 elementary school students left his cafeteria manager "beside herself." Not only did federal pecan purchasing lead to practically force-feeding pecans to schoolchildren, but it pushed orchardists to increase production even further to earn money on the margins, a cycle that was all too common in industrial agriculture. In 1950 U.S. farmers produced 125,622,000 pounds of pecans. A year later, with federal purchases initiated, they produced 143,137,000 pounds. This 13 percent increase was not unusual, but it demanded consistent boosts in consumption.[4]

Pecans went into more than the reluctant mouths of kids at school. For most of American history, pecans were eaten as they were, in unprocessed form and primarily by the handful. Except for pralines, Americans traditionally tended not to include them in desserts, much less in salads or in enchiladas or on fish or as addenda to main courses. Instead, they were accustomed to cracking, possibly roasting, and eating the nuts whole. That's what you did with a pecan. "They are apt," wrote one commentator in 1900, "to be munched at odd hours." One reason they were not munched at all hours may have been that nuts had a reputation for being not only expensive but hard on the digestive system. The USDA had been telling Americans since the late nineteenth century how "nuts, generally speaking, are not indigestible, despite the popular impression to the contrary." Nevertheless, the "popular impression" was hard to shake. It was widely thought that pecans, while fine for eating every now and then, should not occupy a central role in the American diet. The government, having agreed to buy pecans from producers, desperately wanted to alter that common perception. The situation began to change with the onset of what seemed to be an endless stream of pecans in the 1940s. American food would have to find room for these nuts. Desserts—if food writers had any say in the matter—would lead the way. French Americans had been producing pralines in Louisiana since the middle of the eighteenth century. It was not long, however, before American cookbook writers, newspaper food columnists, and chefs started to highlight the potential of pecans as an essential element of every imaginable dessert. Something about the pecan's natural buttery flavor blended well with sweetness. The process of introducing the pecan to the American sweet tooth started with American GIs living overseas, to whom Uncle Sam sent care packages of something called "Pecan caramel Rolls." By 1946, these rare delicacies were being sold in New York City, with the *Times* reporting that the treats were "new to civilians," but "ex-GIs may remember having them in the South Pacific."

With astonishing abruptness, pecans were transformed into a ubiquitous dessert addendum as production increased and prices dropped. In 1947, the *Chicago Daily Tribune* could note, "While only a fifth of the walnut crop goes to bakers, candy manufacturers, and other food processors, over half of the pecan crop goes to these commercial interests." Central to this transition were desserts such as those mentioned in the same article: pecan candy rolls, pecan cakes, and southern pecan pie (more on this soon). A pecan candy roll consisted of sugar, brown sugar, corn syrup, rock salt, and pecans. Essentially the sugars and syrup were mixed and melted, pecans were added, balls were rolled, and the confection was cooked, cooled, and hardened in tin candy molds. Pecan cakes included eggs, butter, sugar, flour, cinnamon, and pecans. Fat and sugar were creamed with the help of an egg yolk; flour, cinnamon, and pecans were mixed in; the concoction was baked, then "cut in squares while hot." They became an extremely popular end to a typical American meat-and-potatoes meal.[5]

It is difficult to convey the diversity and creativity that characterized the pecan-dessert craze in the 1940s and 1950s. It can be said, though, that this diversity and creativity were emblematic of a uniquely American way of eating—one that was not bound by strict culinary traditions and was open to virtually any reasonable (or not) form of innovation. Here is a select list of some the confections created to accommodate the relentless pecan surplus: pecan sticks, pecan muffins, pecan pumpkin pie, pecan loaf, pecan gold cake, pecan cookies, honey pecan pie, orange pecan pie, pecan cookies, pecan bars, pecan pudding, pecan coffee cake, pecan gingerbread, pecan doughnuts, pecan mint mousse, and pecan peach shortcake. This list, of course, could go on for pages, but the key point is that the surplus, complemented as it was by federal promotional efforts, was essential to this important burst of confectionery creativity.

Pecans—not unlike corn today—had to be stuffed into all manner of food. Noting how the "pecan drops in price," food journalist Mary Meade encouraged readers to "employ nuts with a lavish hand." Her article went on to promote whole wheat pecan bread, rice pecan loaf, golden pecan pie, and party pecan rolls. "Cheaper nuts," explained another article, "bring out many tasty recipes," including "pecan loaf." A pecan loaf was made with rice, cracker crumbs, milk, salt, butter, eggs, and chopped pecans. Everything was beaten together and baked in a "small loaf pan." What's notable about so many of these recipes is the emphasis on the nuts' being "cheap."[6]

Amid the dizzying array of pecan-inspired desserts, the American sweet tooth elevated a couple of dishes to something of an iconic status. Pralines would always be deeply associated with New Orleans, where the French started to prepare them as early as the 1720s. They would also be associated with Creole cooking, the flexible culinary style that emerged from that region. The original praline recipes called for almonds or hazelnuts. However, with an abundance of native pecans on hand, French settlers in Louisiana began to substitute "fat Louisiana pecans" for the more traditional nuts. These creolized pralines were sold on the street well into the nineteenth century, and by the twentieth, recipes for them started to appear in best-selling cookbooks. Pralines sold in the United States today typically include pecans, as well as sugar and cream, or evaporated milk. Sometimes vanilla, molasses, caramel, or maple syrup is added. As the pecan-based dessert industry exploded in the 1940s, pralines went along for the ride, with an interesting twist added here and there. A 1947 recipe, for example, used brown sugar, molasses, and vanilla. The author noted that these were the kind of pralines she had recently eaten in New Orleans, where "tourists wandering around the French Quarter buy them and send them out by the dozens to their friends 'up north.'"[7]

The other iconic dessert to come of age in the 1940s and 1950s was pecan pie, a food as closely associated with southern culinary culture as was the praline with Creole New Orleans. It is commonly asserted that the French invented pecan pie after settling New Orleans. As far as I can tell, there is little evidence to support this claim. What we do know is that the first published pecan pie recipes emerged in the late nineteenth century and that in the 1930s, with the invention of Karo Corn Syrup, the pecan pie became a staple of southern tables around the Thanksgiving holiday, hot on the heels of the pecan harvest. Some say that corn syrup gives the dessert that definitive "ooo-ey goo-ey" consistency; others, deeming corn syrup the essence of culinary corruption, opt for honey or maple syrup. In any case, it is not my intention to determine what is "real" pecan pie or who can lay claim to its origin or whether or not corn syrup is all that evil. What matters for our purposes is that pecan pie was elevated from a regional to a national dish with the convergence of corn syrup and pecan surpluses. Recipes began appearing in standard cookbooks such as *The Fannie Farmer Cookbook* and *Joy of Cooking* for the first time in the early 1940s. By the 1950s, virtually every American—north, south, east, or west—had heard of, if not eaten, a dense slice of pecan pie.

What stood out in the 1940s was how widely interpreted pecan pie was. If there had been a conservative version, though, it would have come from Georgia. Specifically, it would have come from the Magnolia Room in Rich's Department Store in downtown Atlanta. The tearoom served a pecan pie so immensely popular that a baker—an African American woman named Callie Williams—was employed full-time six days a week to do nothing but bake pecan pies. In 1948 she pulled 28,960 pecan pies from her oven. According to the *Los Angeles Times*, Williams's "pecan pie formula" was "polished and brought to perfection by a six-days-a-week workout for a quarter of a century." The west coast writer was evidently moved by Williams's southern handiwork. "The recipe," she rhapsodized, "reads like a poem; it eats like a dream." Callie Williams was known for keeping her coveted recipe close to her chest, but "sometimes she breaks down and tells how she does it." She evidently used eggs, butter, flour, vanilla, salt, sugar, dark corn syrup, and, of course, pecans. How she arranged these ingredients nobody seemed to know. In any case, the *Los Angeles Times*, obviously intrigued by the southern flavor of the pecan experience, ended the article by advising, rather bizarrely: "Eat to the strum of banjos."[8]

Clearly, though, chefs were perfectly comfortable veering away from Miss Callie's gold standard for pecan pie into a number of innovative directions. In the 1930s, a Miss Kathleen Armentrout won a national pecan pie competition by dressing up the conventional recipe with orange zest and orange juice. "Honey pecan pie" called for ⅓ cup of "strained honey," while "Texas pecan pie" required "sweet milk." A Louisiana "yam pecan pie," designed by Elizabeth Ann Coit, called for cinnamon, ginger, scalded milk, and a cup of mashed sweet potatoes. A "pecan pumpkin pie" called for canned pumpkin, cinnamon, and ginger. Molasses pecan pie substituted "medium dark molasses" for the corn syrup. And so on. Interpretations, again, seemed to be endless, and the cultural reach of the pecan pie went much further than that of the more tradition-bound praline. By 1959, the most popular dessert at the Coach House, a famous Manhattan eatery off Washington Square Park, was pecan pie. In such ways did pecan pie join the praline and hundreds of other pecan desserts to help ensure that pecans were "absorbed on the home front."[9]

Pecans went into more than desserts. "You wrong a nut," wrote Jane Holt in 1942, "when you assign it an incidental role in a meal." Building on this advice, Americans responded to the wartime abundance of pecans by working them into common entrées and salads. Again, the evidence for this trend was most conspicuous in the food sections of the nation's leading newspapers (food sections being another invention of the 1940s). Mary Meade reminded readers how "just a few chopped pecans may be sauteed in a little margarine or butter to be sprinkled on a green vegetable ready for serving." She added that "green beans, asparagus, sprouts and peas are attractive this way." A luncheon recipe published in the *Los Angeles Times* in 1939 embellished a fresh fruit salad with "butterscotch pecan biscuits," a recipe that called for adding chopped pecans to "pre-packaged biscuit dough and baking." Other dishes popularized during this time included "sweet potatoes with pecans" (which mixed pecans with cornflakes), lamb and pecan salad (chilled with gelatin), whole wheat pecan bread, mashed sweet potatoes with pecans, rice pecan loaf, carrot pecan loaf (with cheese sauce), cauliflower and pecan salad, and plum-orange-pecan soufflé salad.[10] In many ways, these meals were the signature dishes of the postwar American dinner table. Pecans had no trouble fitting in with the broader culinary changes that were already under way.

The frequent association of pecans with the fall holidays, namely Thanksgiving, was a connection made all the more plausible because so many people had, at some point in the not too distant past, participated in a fall pecan harvest. Spiced pecans became a staple at holiday parties, "recipes for autumn" almost always included cups of pecans, "butter toasted pecans" were promoted as a "good solution to the gift problem," and pumpkin pecan pie became a popular dessert on Thanksgiving dinner menus. Nuts in general came to be appreciated as "traditional food of the fall and of the season's important holiday, Thanksgiving."[11] This development, too, helped encourage pecan consumption in the years of abundance after the war. The Pilgrims never ate pecans at Thanksgiving.

Holiday time or not, Americans were regularly eating pecans in their desserts, salads, and entrées by the end of the 1950s. The aristocrat of nuts had become something of a commoner. While the federal government and the nation's leading food writers surely played a central role in helping pecan growers discover a lucrative domestic market for their surfeit of produce, a number of other changes also helped push pecans—traditionally an unappreciated or elusive native food—into American kitchens. Most notably, the first factor was that pecans were increasingly valued for their nutritional worth during an era when Americans began to take personal nutrition seriously. In 1941 Eleanor Roosevelt led an unprecedented National Nutrition Conference for Defense, and two years later the USDA published its first Recommended Dietary Allowances. Nuts did not make it onto the USDA's iconic pyramid, but the fact remains that American consumers were starting to make a more conscious connection between diet and personal health. This growing interest would soon greatly benefit pecans.

Pecans were well positioned to capitalize on virtually any health trend that caught the public's fancy. Writing about America's emerging "nut eating habit" in the *New York Times*, Florence Brobeck commented, "According to dietary experts the habit is a good one." Pecans were not only "rich in fat and protein," but a small handful of them "represent[s] about as much energy food as two slices of white bread or a cup of cooked oatmeal." Americans were about nothing if not energy. Pecans, Brobeck told her readers, were also "generously supplied with copper" and replete with vitamins A, B, and G. Although many Americans believed (and still do) that one could get protein only from animal flesh, Brobeck reminded them that "inasmuch as nuts supply protein, they are considered substitutes for meat." A few years later, Helen Van Pelt Wilson explained in the pages of the same newspaper that nuts were "especially valuable, since nuts were rich in vitamins A, B, and G and their caloric value is also high." The pulp of "two pecans," she added, "equal the 100 calories of a tablespoon of butter and surpass the 70 calories of a medium sized egg." She also touted the pecan's high protein level. Jane Holt drove home the point, calling pecans "protein rich" and "highly concentrated sources of energy." Vegetarians nationwide were delighted.[12]

Nutritionists were undertaking studies to support what was becoming popular wisdom about the health attributes of the pecan. Pecan oil, in particular, appeared to have especially ameliorative qualities. In one study, the oil, when combined with bananas, improved vision and helped weight maintenance in rats. Another study from the same time period suggested that pecans helped the body retain and absorb vitamin A. One comprehensive study undertaken by the University of

Florida Agricultural Experiment Station found pecans to be rich in thiamine, niacin, and riboflavin. There was not a food grown in the state of Florida that had higher levels of riboflavin, a micronutrient critical to the metabolization of fats and carbohydrates. This association of pecans with health eventually took hold in the court of public opinion. And it lasted. As recently as 2007 a pecan industry representative reminded readers of the *Southwest Farm Press* that "pecans are heart healthy, cholesterol-free, and high in antioxidants." His job, he boasted, was "to extol the health benefits" of America's signature nut.[13]

Another reason that pecans were able to reach consumers was that the 1940s were the decade when the mail-order business began to boom. Pecans were especially well suited to this means of sale and transport. As consumers began to bake more regularly with pecans, they found that it was often hard to find them at local grocery stores. Several companies therefore began to make pecans available by air mail. "The nuts may be shipped without difficulty," explained one industry analyst, adding that "spiced pecans" were "being introduced now for just that reason." To obtain them, all one had to do was send a mail-order request to Brownies by Lucille in New York (Lucille and her partner were self-described "professional women who conduct their enterprise after office hours"). Home cooks took ample advantage of such mail-order operations in part because they could order in bulk and store the surplus. The USDA reported that "pecan meats stayed fresh two months at room temperature, nine months at refrigerator temperature, and two years at freezer temperature." Unlike many other foods, nuts—as Americans dating back to the Native Americans well understood—stored well. Refrigerators, of course, worked better than cold caves (I guess).[14]

Mail-order operations, as Brownies by Lucille suggests, were usually homegrown, small-scale endeavors undertaken by women with a personal connection to a pecan source. This was the case for Mrs. Marion Momar, of Cotton Hope Plantation, South Carolina. From the comfort of her home, she "shells and neatly halves pecans, then packs them in a one pound cellophane bag" for mail-order delivery at $1.75, postage included. In that cellophane bag she added "recipes for some of the sweets in which pecans figure prominently— pralines, date pecan pudding, and pecan pie." This was less of a full-time business than an effort to earn, as she put it, "pin money." It was also not unusual for restaurants to rely on mail order. The aforementioned Coach House produced pecan pie nine inches in diameter. It could be ordered "through the mail for $3.50 postpaid." Mail orders played a critical role at a critical time, bridging the gap between producer and consumer before bags of pecans found a permanent place on grocery store shelves, not to mention in the warehouses of cereal makers and ice creameries nationwide. Once these stores did begin to carry bags of pecans—in 1948, for example, when the chain A&P began carrying one-pound bags of un-shelled pecans for 49 cents—the mom-and-pop mail-order operations began to diminish. Familiar story. (Although not totally predictable, as the Great San Saba Pecan Company in San Saba, Texas, which is a small, vertically integrated, and successful company, started in the 1970s and thriving today attests.)[15]

A related development that helped ensure consumer access to a wider array of pecan-based products was the emergence of frozen foods. The first frozen foods sold at retail were vegetables packaged by Birds Eye Frosted Foods. This was in 1930. The Springfield, Massachusetts, company set a trend that is not only with us today more than ever, but swept up pecan products in the 1940s and 1950s. The most common pecan-based delicacy to emerge from the frozen dessert boom was the pecan pie. The prime mover on this score was Hartford's Connecticut Pie Company, founded in 1917. In 1949 the company transitioned from fresh to frozen pies, with its most popular item being the "Southern pecan pie." These frozen disks sold so well that in 1959 the company created a subsidiary called Farm House Frozen Pies. This company distributed frozen pecan pies to grocery stores across the United States, where they sold for under 90 cents each.[16]

As the advent of the frozen pecan pie suggests, an important transition was under way: pecans were increasingly being absorbed by commercial food producers rather than by domestic consumers. This was especially true by the late 1950s and early 1960s. For example, Pepperidge Farm put out two extremely popular items: Butter Pecan Rolls and Cinnamon Pecan Wedges—horrible for one's health, but items that millions of Americans found to be tasty enough to eat regularly. These items came packaged in an aluminum foil tin pan and consumers were advised to heat the items for eight to ten minutes in a 350-degree oven. Not to be outdone, Betty Crocker followed hot on the heels of Pepperidge Farm, offering butter pecan muffin mix in the 1960s. The result was praised by the *Washington Post* as "rich and nutty." Another major commercial supplier of pecan products was the restaurant and candy store chain known as Stuckey's. Started by William Stuckey in 1938 in the small town of Eastman, Georgia, the chain—distinguished by its signature red signs and blue roofs—went on to line highways throughout the country, mostly in the South, where 160 stores consumed massive amounts of pecans, most of them stuffed into pies, and most of them sourced from founder William Stuckey's native state of Georgia.[17]

Commercial developments evolved in tandem with the growing scale of pecan production and distribution. In 1954, the New York–based company Standard Brands, which distributed an array of food products including tea, pudding, yeast, and vodka, purchased the San Antonio–based Southern Pecan Shelling Company. This acquisition, according to the

Wall Street Journal, would likely enable pecans to go large scale, reaching not just home bakers but "candy and ice cream manufacturers and other bulk users." The prediction bore fruit when, seven years later, Standard bought the Curtiss Candy Company, providing direct access to pecans for a variety of popular candies (although the pecan's unusual oiliness prevented it from becoming a common nut in candy bars). In 1963, the Pet Milk Company, which had built a fortune by selling evaporated milk during wartime but, with the fighting over, had recently transformed into a "food products conglomerate," constructed a 75,000-square-foot pecan-processing plant and cold storage warehouse in Albany, Georgia. This move not only affirmed Georgia's status as one of the nation's largest pecan-producing states by the 1960s, but also signaled the pecan's transition into an industrial-scale domestic crop. An additional element of the emerging pecan industry infrastructure was the relentless consolidation of the shelling industry. Between 1945 and 1990, the number of shelling companies diminished nationally from 150 to 22. Consolidation continued unabated, emblematic of the American way of production.[18]

A final aspect of the unusually absorbent domestic market for pecans was the emergence of a wide variety of secondary uses for pecans and pecan by-products. Pecan nut oil became popular as a lubricant in making clocks and guns. Pecan shells were used to oil jet engines. Catholics used pecans to "lend variety to Lenten meals." By the late 1960s and 1970s, pecans had become a central part of an increasingly popular vegetarian diet. Noting that "vegetarianism had become a serious, integral part of America's eating habits," food writer Louis Szathmary promoted pecans as an important source of protein. Other vegetarians—perhaps inadvertently perpetuating the nuts' "crunchy" aspect—became granola fanatics, and pecans became a basic ingredient of the healthy cereal. A recipe for "flamboyant granola" called for a cup of pecans, plus five other kinds of nuts. As the pecan industry grew, a market for pecan wood eventually developed. The most notable use was as flooring for basketball courts. The first court to be installed was at Georgetown University (my alma mater). Declaring that there was "more bounce to the ounce on courts made of pecan," the *New York Times* reported that a pecan court was "desirable for its resiliency." The same might be said for the domestic market that arose to consume the vast surplus of pecans that American eaters had confronted at the beginning of the 1940s.[19]

The national quest to shove pecans into virtually every food product that had a little extra room for stuffing was nothing new to the increasingly consolidating and industrializing American food industry. Corn and soy, as readers of Michael Pollan well know, get processed and jammed into every food item imaginable. Less well known is that the practice of seeking new and varied uses for pecans paralleled the efforts to seek novel and varied uses for crops such as corn and soy well into the late twentieth century. The story recounted in this chapter continued for decades. Indeed, between 1960 and 2000, several pecan-based trends developed to keep American consumers wedded to their native nut.

The most notable of these was the creation of more savory entrées that made pecans the central focus, rather than an addendum to be sprinkled on for garnish right before serving. Pecan-stuffed onions required boiling a large onion, hollowing out the center, stuffing it with a mixture of chopped pecans, bread crumbs, and the part of the onion that had been removed, and baking it "till soft and crumbs are brown." A recipe for "wild rice pecan casserole" instructed the home cook to sauté onions, pecans, garlic, and mushrooms in butter, mix with cooked rice, place in a casserole, and bake. A pecan vegetable loaf that became popular in the 1950s included more than half a cup of pecans per serving. A popular version of pecan potato croquettes was as much pecan as potato. All these recipes were featured in both national newspapers and popular cookbooks, including *Woman's Day Book of Baking*, *New Southern Cooking*, and *Main Courses (Company's Coming)*.[20]

Pecans also began to end up in massively consumed and highly processed items such as ice cream and cereal—two dumping grounds that would prove very popular and profitable for pecan producers and distributors toward the end of the century. Ice cream became a standard destination for pecans with the advent of the industrial-scale "ingredient feeder." The Hoyer RF-SIOO rotary filler was the key. This device could process pecans into 2,400 gallons of ice cream an hour. As a result, the "mix-in business" moved to something of an elevated plateau, a point it had been working to reach since the 1950s, when the Pecan Deluxe Candy Company of Dallas started to supply ice cream shops with "mix in" chopped pecans. By the 1970s, more than seventy shops were using the Pecan Deluxe product. The mechanized ingredient feeder changed the nature of the game. Pecans were no longer mixed in by hand by a high school kid at the corner ice cream shop. Instead they were churned in by an industrial producer such as ConAgra Foods and the ice cream was produced on a gargantuan scale for retail distribution. By the end of the 1990s, every ice cream producer, from generic brands to Godiva, offered one variety or another of pecan ice cream. Butter pecan remains a great favorite among ice cream devotees today.[21]

Pecans went beyond granola in the 1980s and 1990s and found a niche with cereal companies as well. The appeal of pecans to cereal makers was that in an era of obsessive-compulsive nutritional label reading, even a small amount of pecans added a range of beneficial vitamins and minerals that could be championed. The drawback was that in an age of even more obsessive-compulsive calorie counting, the nuts added a big serving of fat (albeit mostly unsaturated). "The best cereals," explained *Consumer Reports*, "give you a good dose of fiber and a little fat." Aiming to strike this balance, companies like Kellogg, General Mills, Quaker Oats, and Post discovered how "indulgent ingredients like pecans" created a "value added cereal" that was extremely popular with consumers. "Taste," explained *Brandweek*, "is especially important to attract and keep" the cereal-eating audience during a period of exploding cereal options, lest (God forbid) the "magic of the cereal aisle begin to wear off."[22]

Another development that sustained pecan consumption well into the late twentieth century was the evolution of the pecan pie from a southern delicacy into an über-Americanized dessert available in grocery freezers nationwide. "It would be difficult," explained *Restaurant Hospitality* in 1998, "to find a more American dessert than pecan pie." This upgrade from "southern" to "American" was excellent news for the producers of pecan pie. The article went on to explain, as we have seen, that "it was corn syrup—specifically the Karo brand corn syrup—that boosted the pecan to national prominence." The dessert might have kept "a decidedly Southern twang," but there was no denying that, as *Nation's Restaurant News* put it, "Nothing sweetens up a menu the way the all-American pecan pie can." Pecan pies were being frozen and sold by mail order. They were being peddled at large grocery store chains. They could be found at gas station convenience stores in Massachusetts. But this loss of regional identity did not keep Elsie Millicent, the great-granddaughter of pecan pioneer E. E. Risien, from baking and delivering a pecan pie to every new resident of San Saba, Texas. They could have put the pie on the American flag and it would have seemed normal to most Americans.[23]

As gourmet cooking—specifically, nouvelle cuisine—began to court the attention of upper-class Americans who wanted to experience French food, the once-aristocratic pecan returned to play an important role. By the late 1980s, high-end chefs began to include pecans in a variety of gourmet-cum-comfort-food dishes. Diners at Stephan Pyles's Star Canyon restaurant in Dallas could find a wild mushroom enchilada with maple-pecan yams. At Bette's Oceanview Diner in Berkeley, California, patrons could order the ideal comfort food—a stack of buttermilk pancakes—but with pecans added to the batter. These kinds of dishes caught on nationally. But by far the most popular pecan-inspired variation was pecan-encrusted fish. This culinary trend was also actively promoted by the government. "Did you know," asked the Bureau of Commercial Fisheries, "that a new romance has developed between ever-popular fish and shellfish, and the North American native, the pecan?"

In Calistoga, California, the noted Louisiana chef Jan Birnbaum—trained by Paul Prudhomme—opened the Catahoula Restaurant and Saloon, where he introduced Californians to pecan-encrusted catfish. Other chefs branched out as well. Alaskan salmon with "pecan crunch coating" started to make its way onto menus in the 1990s, as did "crab and pecan fritters." Mountain trout with a pecan crust became a defining dish to come out of North Georgia. Chefs in places such as Charleston and Savannah began to promote pecan-encrusted catfish as an emblem of traditional southern fare. It was not until the 1990s, however, that this "tradition" became popular.[24]

The end of the twentieth century also witnessed the arrival of a number of miscellaneous pecan-based items. Whether it was pecan-flavored coffee, pecan porter beer, Pecan Sandies and Supremes (both Nabisco innovations), pecan shortbread (Keebler), pecan Danishes, or Texas Chewie Pecan Pralines (ironically, not sold in Texas), the fact remained: American producers were packing pecans into every visible nook and cranny of the American food system. Even pecan shells found wider markets as mulch, barbecue chips, plywood filler, an absorbent for heavy metals, an inert ingredient in pesticides, oil filters, and ink. The annual surpluses of pecans that had begun to glut the market in the 1940s were steadily consumed in the decades that followed. The vast majority of those pecans, moreover, were eaten by American consumers, whose food traditions were flexible enough to incorporate pecans into virtually any dish imaginable, be it sweet, savory, or sour, fresh or frozen, hot or cold. Production and consumption had come into sync. It would not be long, though, before that delicate balance, and the fate of the pecan, shifted yet again. The pecan, ironically, was about to become more popular on the other side of the world than it had ever been at home.

CHAPTER 8

"*China Wants Our Nuts*"

THE PECAN GOES GLOBAL

In the spring of 2011 I visited Berdoll Pecan Farms, located on a gentle bend in the Colorado River in Bastrop, Texas. By contemporary standards the farm is not especially large. The Berdoll family, who purchased the property in 1980, cultivates about 15,000 improved trees, mostly Wichita, Navaho, and Pawnee varieties. As Lisa Berdoll showed me around in her expansive Suburban, I was struck by two things in particular. First, the entire operation is a streamlined model of mechanization. Vehicles designed to fit snugly between seemingly endless rows of perfectly aligned pecan trees spray pesticides, herbicides, and fungicides; they lay mulch, prune trees, apply fertilizer, and harvest nuts. Other machines disk the soil and smooth the turf between trees so that fallen nuts do not elude harvest. At times helicopters are even brought in for the purpose of keeping frost from icing the nuts. Propane cannons are on hand to scare off crows. It occurred to me as we drove from orchard to orchard that there was nothing "natural" about a contemporary pecan orchard. I was looking at a factory in the field.

The second thing that struck me was how the farm makes its money. Berdoll's profits do not come from selling nuts—most of which go two miles down the road to the Berdoll retail outlet located on Highway 71 (and virtually impossible to miss, thanks to its gargantuan red neon sign). Instead, the Berdolls make most of their money from their nursery, which contains about 90,000 trees. They cultivate several varieties of pecans that do well in arid climates and sell the saplings to new orchards being developed in West Texas and New Mexico—the new regional crucible of pecan production in the United States. From the American West the pecans go to China. Indeed, the pecan is now a crop with a global market. How that transition happened, and the impact it has had on pecan production and consumption, brings the story of pecan domestication up to the present moment.

Throughout the 1970s and 1980s, pecan production and consumption in the United States increased by periodic leaps and bounds, all the while keeping close pace with each other. Although the climb was anything but steady, growers increased production from 240 million pounds a year in 1971 to almost 380 million pounds in 1993—a nearly 60 percent gain in output. Pecan acreage in production between 1974 and 1992 increased as well, from 323,000 acres to 462,000 acres—a 42 percent change. Globally, with higher yields per acre, the United States was producing more than 80 percent of the world's pecans, with most of the other 20 percent coming from northern Mexico near the U.S. border. This general market profile was pretty much what any agricultural industry could ask for: supply and demand were well synced, there were no other significant global producers of pecans with which to compete, and crops were mainly free of persistent external threats such as fungi and insects as a result of generally effective chemical agents and strategies of integrated pest management.[1]

By the late 1980s and early 1990s, however, a sharp departure from this customary consumption-supply symbiosis occurred. Supply began to outpace demand. The potential reasons for this growing disparity were numerous. One factor may have been the decision by American cereal makers to switch to walnuts, which experienced a boom in production in the late 1980s and a drop in price. Another may have been the maturation of the unusual number of pecan trees planted in the 1980s that were now reaching commercial levels of production (thus spiking supply in a short span of time). It was also possible that candy makers were starting to choose almonds over pecans because almonds were coming to be thought of as less oily. "Pecans," explained one industry observer in 1994, "bleed through chocolate." It is also possible that the tough economic climate of the early 1990s led many people to gather wild pecans and sell them to suppliers (almost a quarter of commercial nuts in the early 1990s were bought from pecan wildcatters), thereby creating an overall domestic supply of inconsistent quality (this is not to suggest that wild pecans taste worse than domesticated ones; the two simply have different qualities). Some analysts speculated that pecans were losing ground against other nuts because of poor marketing efforts. The pecan industry, after all, was not vertically integrated, and with its relatively weak marketing organizations it could not attract consumers with its version of the dancing peanut equipped with top hat and cane.[2]

Whatever the reason, or combination of reasons, there was no avoiding the conclusion by the middle of the 1990s that the pecan industry had hit a rough patch for the first time in its young history. Industry analysts complained that the pecan was "an infrequent visitor to northern kitchens" and that the pecan business "never got its act together." Others lamented that the pecan was so poorly promoted that all the industry could point to as an example of successful marketing was a shout-out to pecans given by *Today* Show weatherman Willard Scott. The problem, however, had little to do with marketing efforts, or a lack thereof. The problem with the pecan industry, and the underlying cause of its slump, was that the improved pecan was such a newly cultivated nut. While demand had reached a point at which a uniform supply mattered a great deal to processors and commercial consumers alike, pecans had yet to be accordingly standardized. The reason for this divergence was that there were still too many wild pecan trees from which to gather nuts. One report put it this way: "The organized scientific pecan growers have had their impact on the industry, but the input of individuals gathering odd-lots of the nuts in bags and cans remains strong."[3] This input, many believed, would have to be curtailed.

In many ways, though, the commercial bias against the wild pecan was shortsighted. As suggested, the persistence of wild pecans maintained genetic diversity that, in turn, discouraged disease and insect infestation. Wild pecans, moreover, were much less labor-intensive and did not require systematic applications of pesticides. Nevertheless, the heroic strides taken toward rationalized cultivation led industry leaders to believe very deeply that there were still too many farmers who passively cultivated pecans with the same methods employed by their ancestors hundreds of years earlier. These nuts, and the trees that produced them, were, it was thought, starting to disrupt the industry, primarily because the industry had tapped markets for which consistency, uniformity, and predictability— all qualities harder to achieve with wild nuts—now mattered more than ever before. One report described the stream of wild nuts making its way into the commercial pecan supply as marked by "poor kernel fill, rancidity, excessive particles and dust, and dark color." It should be noted that this was a novel problem. It was hard to find another commodity in which fruit from farms with tens of thousands of top-quality cultivars was intermixed with fruit from wild relatives picked by scratch farmers. For most of the cultivated pecan's history, such intermixing was inconsequential, if not beneficial for the industry as a whole. Now, however, the consequences were obvious. Producers were caught unprepared.[4]

As the market for pecans expanded, wild pecans started to create trouble for reasons beyond their own collective inconsistency. When the high-end cultivars grown on mechanized farms were mixed with wild pecans—as they always were for distribution purposes—the results could cause difficulty downstream in the supply chain. Wild nuts, the diverse products of nature, were harder to sort and grade in a human-designed system since they often did not conform to grading gauges. Wild trees were also more likely to mast inconsistently, making it difficult for marketers to predict supply—something that was much easier to do when you could count cultivars planted and make estimates based on established annual masting records. The mixture of wild and cultivated nuts had the added effect of driving up prices for some commercial consumers while depressing them for others. Consumers who demanded the highest-quality pecans—say, makers of frozen pecan pies—would have to pay more because shellers would store and sell the cultivated pecans separately from their wild cousins. Those who could get away with using wild pecans—namely ice cream makers—would enjoy prices based on the overall, rather than the cultivated, cost of pecans, thereby lowering returns to farmers. This inconsistency made the industry a "highly speculative" one for agricultural investors. Finally, wild pecans—because they were not sprayed—were more susceptible to fungal outbreaks that could not only further destabilize supply but also pose a threat to cultivated varieties.[5]

For all these reasons, by the late 1990s industry observers were anything but optimistic about the future of the American pecan industry. "The pecan market," predicted the trade journal *Candy Industry* in 1994, "will continue to remain soft and prices are declining." Two years later, a report by the

USDA's Economic Research Service came to the same conclusion, explaining, "Pecan prices are likely to remain weak." Meanwhile, efforts to keep wild nuts out of the supply chain came to naught. When the Pecan Marketing Board initiated an effort to tax wild nuts entering the supply chain, local pecan wildcatters erupted in outrage. One resident of San Saba, Texas—the veritable epicenter of wild pecan groves—told the *Wall Street Journal* that, although she wanted to support the tax, "there would probably be 10 pickups trying to run me over" if she did. Given this response, one could have looked at the pecan industry in the 1990s and concluded that it had had its run and that the pecan was a crop best left to sow its wild oats and revert to its uncultivated status.[6] Many people thought that was exactly what should have happened.

An optimistic observer of the industry during the dark times of the 1990s might have surmised that two things needed to happen in order for the pecan business to recover and thrive. First, given the fluctuations in price and supply, new markets, preferably large foreign ones, would have to open up. Second, under export pressure, pecan growers would have to start supplying shellers and distributors with more-uniform batches of nuts. All of this would seem to have been wishful thinking. Remarkably, however, that's exactly what did happen. Few analysts could possibly have predicted, even in their most glass-half-full moments, that the market that would eventually emerge to rescue pecans—China's exploding middle class—would be the largest market imaginable. Nor could they have predicted that the region of the United States that would move to supply the Chinese market—namely, the arid western portion of the country—would lack wild varieties altogether, thus necessitating a supply of consistently improved varieties and an industry that to this day is booming as a result of an immensely popular and profitable China connection.

A market as lucrative as China does not fall into an industry's lap. Efforts to reach export markets began in earnest in the mid-1980s. The Southern United States Trade Association and the Western United States Agricultural Trade Association (USDA programs) began to actively promote pecans in European markets, especially in the United Kingdom and Germany. These efforts included $490,000 in funding from the Targeted Export Assistance Program (also a USDA program) and another $1.5 million from the Farmers Market Promotion Program. A modest contribution, $233,329, also came from the Market Access Program. These funds helped to support a tentative entrance into European markets, especially the UK and Germany. Despite these efforts, most pecan exports still went to Canada and Mexico (primarily to be shelled and sent back to the United States) until the 2000s. The vast majority of pecans continued to be consumed where they had always been consumed: on the home front. Writing in 1998, one analyst noted that "pecan exports have experienced slow growth and are a minor share of supply," about 20 percent. For a variety of reasons—but mainly because almonds and walnuts were cheaper and more appreciated in Europe—the European market would always remain a tough nut to crack for pecan exporters.[7]

Another market that U.S. pecan producers tentatively tapped was Japan's. With Hong Kong imposing no restrictions on pecan imports, that city served as a logical re-export point to Japan, where pecans had become something of a delicacy since they were first introduced in the 1970s. Even with Japan's rising middle class and growing population, though, pecans were never able to do any better there than they did in Europe. The higher classes enjoyed them as a complement to tea, but interest from the population at large was low. Commenting on the lack of popularity of pecans in Japan, the president of the Toyo Nut Company in Kobe said, "It's like horse racing; almonds, walnuts, and pistachios are already ahead." The supply-demand disparity that came about in the 1990s thus persisted into the early twenty-first century, with these initial efforts coming to naught.[8]

The big break into the China market by the United States took place at a 2006 trade show in Paris. It was then that an official from New Mexico's Department of Agriculture, on a lark, introduced a team of buyers from China to a batch of large, unshelled pecans. The Chinese cracked them open, sampled them, and were intrigued—so intrigued that they traveled to New Mexico to meet growers, tour orchards, and discuss tentative contracts. New Mexico pecans appealed to the Chinese because, as one report put it, "the quality from natives isn't as good as the improved varieties that make up all of New Mexico's crop." In other words, the Chinese—no matter what the consequences for the American nut—wanted cultivated nuts. After the Chinese visit to New Mexico, the director of marketing for the state's agriculture department told a Lubbock, Texas, newspaper, "We think there's potential for tremendous growth." That turned out to be an understatement. Three years later, the Chinese were consuming more than a third of the 315 million pounds of pecans harvested by New Mexico farmers.[9]

This "explosive consumer demand," as one trade industry magazine put it, was unprecedented in any industry, much less in the inchoate pecan business. The statistics tell the story of a rapid change in fortune for an industry that had fallen into the doldrums. In 2000, China did not even have a word for "pecan." The country imported no pecans; no one ate them. In 2003, China imported less than a million pounds of pecans. In 2008, a year after the United States had a bumper crop of pecans amid a worldwide shortage of walnuts, the Chinese purchased 53 million pounds of pecans. The following year they bought 83 million pounds—out of a total of 300 million pounds produced in the United States. This amount was more than all other pecan exports combined. Between 2009 and 2010, pecan exports leapt by 61 percent, with more than half of U.S. exports going directly to China. The trend dipped a bit in 2011, but generally looks to continue strong. In 2005 China accounted for less than 1 percent of the overall U.S. crop; in 2011 it bought 27 percent of the U.S. crop. New Mexico, which benefited the most from the Chinese market, watched exports go from 600,000 pounds in 2005 to 15 million pounds in 2010.[10]

Growers were, and continue to be, thrilled with this turn of events. Prices of pecans skyrocketed under the pressure of Chinese demand. Georgia orchardists—who mostly produce improved varieties—were actively courted by Chinese importers. "The Chinese," explained one newspaper report, "have been cold-calling even small growers to obtain supplies." This was no overstatement. "A month before harvest," said one grower, "your e-mail fills up, you get phone calls. One of our best Chinese customers called my partner at 2 a.m. looking for nuts." Pecan prices obviously went haywire. With the Chinese middle class willing to pay $10 to $15 a pound for large, unshelled pecans, prices on the domestic front were bound to spike. In 2008 pecans were retailing around $3.50 per pound. By 2010 the price was at $6.95. In 2011, one could easily come across bags of shelled pecans selling for $9.30 a pound. The value of pecan orchards rose from a range of $3,000-$3,800 an acre to $4,500-$6,000. For those on the right side of this boom, times had changed. "It's a good thing," said the owner of one New Mexico pecan farm. "It's a very good thing."[11]

The Chinese interest in pecans was driven not only by a decline in the global walnut supply and the emergence of a Chinese middle class with enough disposable income to splurge more than occasionally on $9 bags of pecans. China was undergoing something of a health craze as well, and pecans were widely recognized for their health benefits. "We used to eat walnuts," explained one Chinese woman to a reporter, "and then we saw on TV that pecans were more nutritious than walnuts." She added, "Pecans are very good for the brain, and we older people should eat more pecans so that we don't get Alzheimer's." A New Mexico grower, when asked to speculate on this explosion in Chinese demand, explained that the pecan is a great-tasting nut, adding (about the Chinese), "They also think it's very healthy for you." The pecan industry was diligent about playing up this aspect of the nut. A former head of the Georgia Pecan Growers Association reminded Chinese consumers: "as healthy as the pecan is, as the number one nut in antioxidants, you'd have to eat three times the amount of almonds to compare to pecans." The Chinese had a unique way of eating pecans: they partially cracked the nuts, soaked them in brine, and roasted them, eating them like others eat pistachios. "The pecan," explained one somewhat bemused U.S. pecan importer, "has become associated with longevity."[12]

The Chinese market transformed the American pecan industry in less than a decade. In 2005 pecans were a novelty item in China. Today they can be found, as one newspaper reports, "at gas stations, airports, and every grocery store in China." The impact of hundreds of millions of new consumers suddenly swarming to consume American pecans is hard to capture in its entirety, but a few changes stand out. First, China's demand for large pecans of uniform quality meant that states with wild pecans—such as Texas and Louisiana, which once dominated the industry—quickly lost ground to states that grew only cultivated varieties, such as Georgia, Arizona, and New Mexico. Second, because the Chinese demanded pecans in the shell and imported them directly through Vietnam (to save on direct import costs), shellers and distributors in the United States also fell on hard times. The pecan industry is not and never has been vertically integrated, leaving the downstream components of the industry especially vulnerable to Chinese demand. Third, the dominance of the Chinese market drove up the price of pecans at home. As a result, not only home consumers but also the industries that spent the 1960s and 1970s turning cheap chopped pecans into every food possible—ice cream, pies, muffins, etc.—were being priced out of the pecan market. As America's native crop boomed, Americans were eating less and less of their own homegrown nut. Today you do not find pecans in processed foods nearly as often as you once did.

Industry leaders have expressed considerable angst about this last development. Assessing the meteoric rise in pecan prices, Jeff Worn, vice president of the South Georgia Pecan Company, a distributor to Russell Stover and Sara Lee, has been the most outspoken about the dangers of yielding too much market share to the Chinese. "In an already suffering economy," he wondered, "how long will people be able to pay that much for pecans?" Speaking on *CNN Money*, Worn continued, "Pecans are a staple here in the United States and I hope that with current household income under pressure we don't price ourselves out of the market." In the spirit of this concern, several growers declared their loyalty to their domestic clients. As a Texas grower told the *Fort Worth Star-Telegram*, "I'm very keen on keeping it local." The idea of the local certainly has great sway, but at the end of the day, it seemed that another kind of logic had prevailed. One giddy Texas grower explained to the *Wall Street Journal* where and when he would sell: "I'm going to wait," he declared, "till the price gets higher."[13]

Another reason that many observers are wary of alienating domestic consumers as the industry becomes addicted to Chinese demand is that the Chinese, who are currently buying agricultural land throughout East Africa, could always start building their own pecan orchards. They do, after all, have more than a passing familiarity with locally grown Asian hickories. While it would take decades for them to even come close to matching American levels of pecan production, the possibility nonetheless remains that the Chinese could viably pursue pecan production. It is perhaps for this reason that American pecan marketers are trying to stay a step ahead of the game by exploring a potentially even more lucrative market: India. Jeff Worn might have been genuinely concerned about protecting the domestic market from skyrocketing pecan prices as a result of foreign demand, but he was not going to miss out on the emergence of another potentially huge overseas market. In July 2011 National Public Radio found Worn after he had attended a trade show in India, where he was hoping to introduce pecans. "We were cooking pecans with rice and things like that at the booth," he explained. "And people really ate it up."[14]

The China connection, as well as an impending India connection, highlights a bittersweet reality for the pecan industry. For better or worse, survival in the commercial pecan business now depends on managing increasingly expansive orchards with ironclad efficiency to meet broadening market demand. Without the presence of substantial wild nuts, humans, through careful methods of management, must work to expand scope, minimize the vagaries of nature, routinize the processes of production, and transform orchards into the outdoor equivalent of assembly lines. One could argue that the process of bending nature to the will of humans to meet market demand has been happening with pecans since the origin of Antoine's grafted Centennial pecan. That would be true.

It is important, however, to recall that the relatively short history of commercial pecan production has always been marked by a healthy mixture of the wild and the domesticated. Traditionally, states where pecan production was the highest were states endowed with millions upon millions of wild pecan trees. These states, armed with such an ample sampling of wild stock, were also the states where the earliest cultivars were developed (Texas and Louisiana). It is easy to lose sight of the point that the coexistence of wild and cultivated pecans had a quiet way of tempering the drive toward industrialization, highlighting respect for the native landscape, and encouraging the use of integrated pest management rather than systematic spraying. The opening of the Chinese market, however, threatens to make even vestiges of the wild/cultivated coexistence obsolete. It provides a powerful push in the already intensifying trend toward the exclusive production of improved varieties through methods that are entirely and rigidly mechanized, regrettably intolerant of the diverse vagaries marking wild pecans.

The result, as my visit to Berdoll Farms suggested, was an approach to agricultural production predicated on minimizing the impact of natural processes—weed growth, insect proliferation, fungal outbreaks, declines in soil quality—and maximizing the efficiency of domesticated pecan production. Put differently, the result was the rapid evolution of orchards that stood in the starkest possible contrast to the earliest passively cultivated orchards—orchards where weeds, diseases, and insects were, with few exceptions, left to interact on their own terms, or managed through cultural controls that mimicked the actions of the natural world. Humans, rather than nature, now micro-manage every stage of production. Production, moreover, has become an almost exclusively chemically saturated activity. The kind of monoculture practiced by mammoth orchards producing hundreds of thousands of pounds of nuts a year opened unprecedented opportunities for disease, insect, and weed outbreaks. These potential outbreaks were consistently met with, as they have been throughout contemporary agriculture, chemical agents that when applied injudiciously exact damages on human health and the environment.

I'm speaking generally, but consider what pecan growers typically spray for the purposes of weed control alone. Before planting saplings, growers broadcast a mitosis inhibitor to prevent the sprouting of grasses and small-seeded broadleaf weeds. Before the emergence of pecans, up to eight different kind of "preemergence" herbicides are sprayed, most of them photosynthesis and cellulose inhibitors designed to suffocate succulent weed seedlings. Then comes the "postemergence" onslaught, which could include a dozen agents (paraquat, glyphosate) notable not only for their effectiveness but also for the warnings they elicit. "DO NOT allow livestock to graze treated areas," "DO NOT harvest within 30 days of treatment," and "DO NOT apply within two weeks of budbreak" are labels affirming the cost of minimizing the rhythms of nature to achieve maximum levels of production. Herbicides with muscular names such as Goal, Rage, Fusilade, and Firestorm were adopted in an effort to combat weeds such as goosegrass, ragweed, pigweed, nutsedge, lamb's-quarter, crabgrass, and morning glory.[15]

Orchardists can do many things to minimize pest infestations—prune low-hanging stems, clear debris, keep weeds down, plant vetches to promote beneficial insects. Many do these things as part of a larger integrated pest-management approach. Chemicals will always have the most appeal to most growers, especially as the cost of control stabilizes while pecan prices increase. The pecan is under constant threat from the pecan weevil, the pecan nut casebearer, stinkbugs, spittlebugs, aphids, webworms, walnut caterpillars, spider mites, pecan phylloxera, Asian ambrosia beetles, and the red imported fire ant. While concerted efforts have been under way for decades to employ the less chemically reliant methods of integrated pest management, orchardists who are typically attuned to annual economic cycles find it most convenient and effective to reach for the big guns. Malathion, Sevin, and a number of pyrethroids and organophosphates are routinely used to fight major pests in pecan orchards. These agents might protect nuts well, but they threaten bees, birds, fish, and other wildlife that are unfortunate enough to wander into the insecticide fog. Committing to the industrial production of a handful of improved cultivars for markets demanding high volume and consistent quality has, for most pecan orchardists, entailed the adaptation of an intricate and systematically pursued spraying schedule.[16]

The process of minimizing the impact of natural processes on orchards extends to the ongoing effort to control the spread of plant diseases as well. Pathogens that have a tendency to attack dense groves of cultivated pecans are highly adaptive to fungicides, thus forcing farmers to rely on an array of agents to outwit, however temporarily, an array of specific diseases. Diseases to be controlled include leaf scab, nut scab, downy spot, and vein spot. Doing so requires up to a dozen applications every season—and more if rains are frequent—of several acetates and organotin compounds. These agents work well, but only when intricate spraying schedules, designed to avoid resistance, are adhered to. Instructions can be maddeningly complex. For example, "Note also that for resistance management, growers planning to use combination products like Stratego, Quilt or Absolute later in the season should limit their use of Sovran or any stand-alone triazole since the combinations contain both of those chemistries. These pre-pollination options fit best where other chemistries like Tin or Elast are used post-pollination." Such is the language of most commercial pecan farming today.[17]

A final area of pecan production requiring constant chemical monitoring involves the soil. Pecans do a relatively good job, largely as a result of an extensive root system, of acquiring ample amounts of phosphorous and potassium on their own. They are less effective, however, when it comes to nitrogen, zinc, calcium, and magnesium, mainly because these nutrients do not exist in the proper ratio in the soil. Fertilization is therefore essential to commercial-scale production. Pecan nuts are dependent on pecan leaves, because the leaves provide the shoots upon which pecan clusters are born. Nutrients make their way into leaves, nine to thirteen of which are required to produce a single cluster of nuts. What makes the process of fertilizing so time-consuming and labor-intensive is the fact that the trees need different nutrients at different stages of their seasonal growth cycle. Thus in one season a farmer will typically apply nitrogen twice in July and August, zinc four times in the spring, potassium whenever soil testing reveals a deficiency, and phosphorous once before planting. Several cover crops such as barley, legumes, and clover could improve soil quality and enhance the absorption of these nutrients. Many pecan farmers employ this technique.

This overview of the complexity of the modern cultivated pecan orchard overlooks more than it captures. Farmers also have to clean and store harvest equipment, deal with irrigation and drainage, monitor insect appearances, graft, keep orchard floors free of debris, do battle with squirrels and crows and raccoons, stay in touch with wholesale and retail buyers, sort through the harvest to cull flawed nuts, winterize engines, sprayers, and irrigation pumps, and—yes—even stand guard against post-harvest pecan poachers. Nuts at $11 a pound have been known to inspire criminality.

Pecans had been leading up to this industrialized point for some time. From the initial transition to improved varieties in the 1920s, to the spike in production during World War II, to the demand generated by candy and cereal companies in postwar America, producers of pecans, perhaps inevitably, steadily manipulated every aspect of the crop's growth to consistently produce more nuts on less land. If the march toward the industrial production of what would become a global commodity took decades, the last five years of Chinese demand have sealed the pecan's fate as a thoroughly industrialized crop. Pecans are now more manufactured than grown, or allowed to grow. There is little doubt that the productive mechanical and chemical technologies driving orchards today have allowed growers in thirteen American states to make pecans available throughout the world. The cost, however (for those who care to dwell on it), is the removal of more and more pecans from the ecosystems that we tend to think of as natural, the kind of environments in which wild pecan groves once thrived, yielding trees of the kind that so enthralled the likes of Gilbert White and the kind that grows through my backyard deck.

Reflecting the commercial perspective on the transition of pecans from a wild to a domesticated crop was Lisa Berdoll, who was introduced at the beginning of this chapter. At one point in my tour, after driving through row after row of neatly aligned, intensively managed pecan trees, we came to the Colorado River, on the banks of which sat a grove of stunning wild pecans. I commented on how beautiful they were—so different-looking, so much more free-form and, well, *wild*-looking than the carefully situated and manicured cultivars. Lisa agreed. Then she explained that they were getting ready to clear them in order to plant a new field of domestic trees.

The Future of Pecans

From the moment of Antoine's graft to this day, the pecan has moved in time and space along a continuum ranging from wild to cultivated. The benefit of this continuum, especially the middle portions of it, is that it allowed pecan growers to make available to consumers a delicious product of nature at an accessible price while at the same time preserving the tree's genetic diversity and general resistance to disease and infestation. Over a hundred-year period, as a result of this balance, the pecan industry generally benefited from the productive coexistence of wild and cultivated pecan trees. The cultivated pecans were marked by consistency and traits tailored to enhance yields in specific environments. The wild ones were correspondingly marked by genetic diversity and a relationship with natural surroundings that allowed them to produce tasty nuts without systematic chemical intervention. Several factors—the emergence of extensive foreign demand, the availability of an ever-specializing chemical arsenal, the expansion of pecan production into regions without native stock, and the land-use threat to native stock—have helped rapidly push the pecan toward the domesticated end of the continuum. The consequences of this shift warrant a brief reflection of what the future holds for the pecan tree in the United States.

It's not a happy prospect. Not to overstate matters, but we could be looking into the face of a perfect storm, one that threatens the pecan's very existence. There are three parts to this scenario that, if they ever converge, may mean that the pecan's only future home will indeed be in a seed bank.

First, consider the current status of wild pecans. In 1919 virtually all of Texas's pecans came from native trees. At some point in the 1990s, after decades of the development of cultivars, the percentage of Texas pecans coming from wild trees dipped below 50 percent—and that figure is still declining today. Although these trees are still productive, it is important to note that wild ecosystems are as fragile as they have ever been. Native groves, moreover, have a limited life span (a typical wild tree might live for 250 years). The wild pecan groves that remain in Texas exist on land that could easily—and one might say will assuredly—be put to more "productive" uses. History pretty much dictates that such a transition is inevitable. There is, therefore, good reason to hypothesize the virtual elimination of wild pecans from Texas, not to mention from the entire United States, in the not too distant future. At best, these trees currently exist in a kind of purgatory, thinned to the point that they can no longer reproduce at the rate at which they need to in order to live long enough to die a natural death. Think about how many times you've seen a lone pecan tree sitting in the middle of a pasture providing shade for cattle. That's a living fossil.

The second part of the scenario involves the cultivars. We can certainly take some solace, as wild stocks decline, in the proliferation of cultivated pecans across the American South and West. Indeed, as long as humans choose to propagate the pecan, it will reliably thrive in American orchards. But these are essentially commercial products, not integral aspects of a natural ecosystem. We therefore have to ask a troubling question: what would happen if the cost of preserving this commercial product began to outweigh the economic return that it provided? In this sense, the future of the cultivated pecan depends on nothing so fickle and precarious as economics. With competition for the global palate coming from related products such as walnuts, almonds, and pistachios, there is good reason to view the current Chinese boom in demand, and the potential India market, as just another trend, nothing more.

Finally, and closely related to the second concern, the heavily chemical-driven approach to disease and insect control that has dominated pecan orchard keeping is leading to increasing levels of insect and disease resistance. This resistance, in turn, is becoming harder and—key point—more expensive to evade, making it more costly to grow pecans. The danger is most evident in the yellow aphid menace. The yellow aphid is generally not a threat to wild pecans, primarily because its presence is countered by spiders and other natural enemies alerted to the aphid's arrival by the conspicuous sap it produces. The overuse of pesticides on cultivated varieties of pecans, however, has led to a decline in natural enemies and the emergence of aphid resistance soon thereafter. Resistance will have to be met with new and often more expensive chemicals. This cycle has been spinning for a long time. In the 1980s, for example, the head of the Federated Pecan Growers predicted that the entire industry was in trouble if pesticide-resistant aphids continued to proliferate. Industry responded by adopting a more potent aphicide. However, within the last few years, this pesticide has started to fail. Aphids have figured out how to get around this one as well. And thus the cost of growing pecans is likely to increase even more, edging growers imperceptibly closer to that fateful tipping point that drives them out of the business, consigning the cultivated pecan to the same fate as the wild one, ending the symbiosis they long enjoyed.

As the invisible hand of nature has yielded to the aggressive hand of humanity, the prospect of this convergence taking place has become that much more likely. In this respect, the pecan, a tree that has lived a truly unique life, one marked by remarkable individuality, may take a depressingly conventional path into obscurity. As the genetic diversity of this remarkable specimen declines, as it becomes increasingly vulnerable to an attack that no chemical can repel, we may very well lose yet another natural thread to the past, one that binds us to native American foragers, Jeffersonian tinkerers, slave gardeners, and, more important than all these, our own sense of place in the natural world that Gilbert White so deeply understood. It is for this reason that I no longer ignore the beautiful tree that grows through my deck.

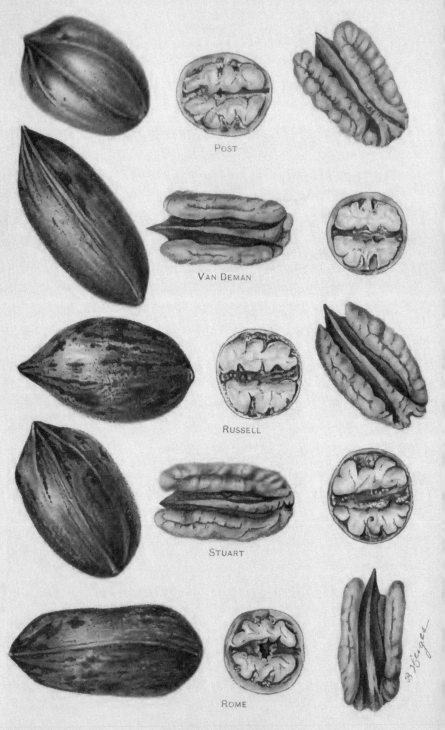

POST

VAN DEMAN

RUSSELL

STUART

ROME

PECAN VARIETIES.

NOTES

INTRODUCTION

1. Richard W. Wrangham, W. C. McGrew, Frans B. M. de Waal, and Paul Heltne, eds., *Chimpanzee Cultures* (Cambridge, MA: Harvard University Press, 1996).

2. L. J. Grauke and Tommy E. Thompson, "Pecans and Hickories," in *Fruit Breeding*, vol. 3, *Nuts*, ed. Jules Janick and James N. Moore (New York: Wiley, 1996); http://www.enotes.com/food-encyclopedia/nuts.

3. For a general discussion of the human-plant relationship, see Michael Pollan, *The Botany of Desire: A Plant's-Eye View of the World* (New York: Random House, 2002); for a more in-depth treatment, see Noel Kingsbury, *Hybrid: The History and Science of Plant Breeding* (Chicago: University of Chicago Press, 2011).

4. Matt Warnock Turner, *Remarkable Plants of Texas* (Austin: University of Texas Press, 2009), 11.

5. Stuart Pecan Company, *The Pecan and How to Grow It* (Chicago: Women's Temperance Publishing Association, 1893), 180–183; Turner, *Remarkable Plants of Texas*, 11; Roger Tory Peterson, *A Field Guide to Eastern Forests* (New York: Houghton Mifflin, 1998), 107.

6. Luther Burbank, "Pecans," in *How Plants Are Trained to Work for Man*, vol. 11 (New York: F. F. Collier and Son, 1914), 144.

7. Darrell Sparks, "Adaptability of Pecan to Its Native Range," *Horticultural Science* 40: 1175–1189; Jean Richardson Flack, "The Spread and Domestication of the Pecan (*Carya illinoensis*) in the United States" (PhD diss., University of Wisconsin, 1970).

8. Flack, "The Spread and Domestication of the Pecan," 23.

9. Grant D. Hall, "Pecan Food Potential in Prehistoric North America," *Economic Botany* 54, no. 1 (2000): 104.

CHAPTER 1

1. Marc D. Abrams and Gregory J. Nowacki, "Native Americans as Active and Passive Promoters of Mast and Fruit Trees in the Eastern USA," *The Holocene* 18, no. 7 (November 2008): 1123–1137.

2. Elias Yanovsky, *Food Plants of the North American Indians*, USDA Miscellaneous Publication 237 (Washington, DC: U.S. Government Printing Office, 1936), 137.

3. Modern Americans, one might note, similarly benefit. Current medical research highlights the health advantages of eating pecans in moderation. The *Journal of Nutrition* explains that switching to a diet in which 40 percent of fat comes from pecans can lead to significantly reduced levels of both "bad" and overall cholesterol. The journal *Nutrition Research* adds that even a handful of pecans daily can reduce the risk of coronary heart disease. According to the *Journal of Agriculture and Food Chemistry*, pecans contain more antioxidants that any other nut on the market. For vegans and vegetarians, pecans are an invaluable resource. One serving contains roughly the same protein as an ounce of meat. http://www.ilovepecans.org/nutrition.html#protectmind; http://happy nutritionist.com/pecans.html; James A. Duke, *Handbook of Nuts* (New York: CRC Press, 1988), 69.

4. D. H. Usner, "A Cycle of Lowland Forest Efficiency: The Late-Archaic Woodland Economy of the Lower Mississippi," *Journal of Anthropological Research* 39, no. 4 (Winter 1983): 434–437; Lyman Carrier, *The Beginnings of Agriculture in America* (New York: Johnson Reprint Corp., 1968), 1–15; http://hubpages.com/hub/Food-native-to-the-Americas -part-2-a-little-less-known. The brewery is the Abita Brewery.

5. John C. Kricher and Gordon Morrison, *A Field Guide to Eastern Forests: North America* (New York: Houghton Mifflin Harcourt, 1998), 107.

6. http://www.lsuagcenter.com/en/our_offices/research_stations /Pecan/Features/Pecan_FAQs/index_seriespage-7.htm.

7. For Native American adherence to the cycles of their ecological systems, see William Cronon, *Changes in the Land: Indians, Colonists, and the Ecology of New England* (New York: Hill and Wang, 1983); also see Paul A. Delcourt and Hazel R. Delcourt, *Prehistoric Native Americans and Ecological Change: Human Ecosystems in Eastern North America since the Pleistocene* (Cambridge, UK: Cambridge University Press, 2004).

8. Hall, "Pecan Food Potential in Prehistoric North America," 107.

9. Flack, "The Spread and Domestication of the Pecan," 55–58.

10. Jane Manaster, *Pecans: The Story in a Nutshell* (Austin: University of Texas Press, 1994; republished by Texas Tech University Press, 2008), 14.

11. Larry N. Brown, "Sex Ratio Bias among Grey Squirrels Foraging at a Single Attractive Seasonal Food Source," *Journal of Mammalogy* 67, no. 3 (1986): 582–583.

12. Roy Bedichek, *Adventures with a Texas Naturalist* (Austin: University of Texas Press, 1975), 128.

13. William E. Hoffmann, "The Relation of the Crow to Pecan Culture," *Wilson Bulletin* 36, no. 4 (1924): 180–182.

14. S. B. Vander Wall, "The Evolutionary Ecology of Nut Dispersal," *Botanical Review* 67, no. 1 (January-March 2001): 80–95.

15. T. R. Adkins, "The Red-headed Woodpecker Occasionally Wintering in Alabama," *Wilson Bulletin* 38, no. 3 (1926): 161.

16. L. E. Yeager and R. G. Rennels, "Fur Yields and Autumn Food of the Raccoons in Illinois River Bottomlands," *Journal of Wildlife Management* 7 (1943): 45–52.

17. John K. Strecker, "Notes on the Texas Cotton and Attwater Wood Rats in Texas," *Journal of Mammalogy* 100, no. 3 (1929): 216–220.

18. Hall, "Pecan Food Potential," 108.

19. J. D. Speth and K. A. Speilmann, "Energy Source, Protein Metabolism, and Hunter-Gatherer Subsistence Strategies," *Journal of Anthropological Archaeology* 2, no. 1 (1983): 1–31; William Caire, Jack D. Tyler, Bryan P. Glass, and Michael A. Mares, *Mammals of Oklahoma* (Norman: University of Oklahoma Press, 1989); Hall, "Pecan Food Potential," 110.

20. Joshua Gorman, "Building a Nation: Chickasaw Museums and the Construction of History and Heritage" (PhD diss., University of Memphis, 2009).

CHAPTER 2

1. The classic text on this topic is Alfred Crosby, *The Columbian Exchange: Biological and Cultural Consequences of 1492* (Westport, CT: Greenwood, 1972).

2. Alan Davidson, ed., *The Oxford Companion to Food* (New York: Oxford University Press, 1999), 592.

3. Jeff Ball, "The Tasty Pecan," *American Forests* 107, no. 3, http://findarticles.com/p/articles/mi_m1016/is_3_107/ai_84053639/.

4. Davidson, *The Oxford Companion to Food*, 833.

5. Edward Wilber Berry, *Notes on the Geological History of the Walnuts and Hickories* (Washington, DC: U.S. Government Printing Office, 1914).

6. Andrew Jackson Downing, *The Fruits and Fruit Trees of America* (New York: John Wiley and Sons, 1859), 261.

7. Patrick Malcolm, "History of Walnuts," http://thephantom writers.com/free_content/db/m/history-of-walnuts.shtml; Oscar Bin-

ner, *Luther Burbank: His Methods and Discoveries and Their Practical Application*, vol. II (Burbank: CA: Burbank Society, 1915), 144.

8. Charles Henry Snow, *The Principal Species of Wood: Their Characteristic Properties* (New York: Wiley, 1908), 57; *Daily Gazette*, January 28, 1874; R. Sidney Boone, Donna Christensen, and Debra Squire, "Wood Species Guide," *Furniture Design and Manufacturing* (December 1988); http://www.fs.fed.us/database/feis/plants/tree/carill/all.html.

9. Londa Schiebinger, *Plants and Empire: Colonial Bioprospecting in the Atlantic World* (Cambridge, MA: Harvard University Press, 2004).

10. Rodney Howard True, "Notes on the Early History of the Pecan in America," in the *Annual Report of the Board of Regents*, 72 (Washington, DC: Smithsonian Institution, 1919); Cecil Gregg, *Pecans for Central Texas: The Establishment, Management, and Care of Pecans in the Area of San Marcos, Texas* (San Marcos: Southwest Texas State University Press, 1975), 1.

11. Hall, "Pecan Food Potential in Prehistoric North America," 107.

12. Ibid.; True, "Notes," 139; Manaster, *Pecans*, 16.

13. William C. Foster and Jack Jackson, eds., "The 1693 Expedition of Governor Salinas Varona to Sustain the Missionaries among the Tejas Indians," *Southwestern Historical Quarterly* 97 (October 1993): 286, 288, 289.

14. True, "Notes," 439–440.

15. J. J. McVey, *Bartram's Garden* (Philadelphia: John Bartram Association, 1907), 13; William P. Corsa, *Nut Culture in the United States: Embracing Native and Introduced Species* (Washington, DC: U.S. Government Printing Office, 1896); also see Nancy Hoffmann and John C. Van Horne, *America's Curious Botanist: A Tercentennial Appraisal of John Bartram, 1699-1777* (Memoirs of the American Philosophical Society, 2004).

16. True, "Notes," 441.

17. Ibid.

18. Ulysses P. Hedrick and Elizabeth Woodburn, *A History of Horticulture in America to 1860* (Portland: Timber Press, 1988), 204.

19. True, "Notes," 446; "Savannah Grown Pecans," October 29, 1886; http://www.mountvernon.org/visit/plan/index.cfm/pid/642/; Ulysses P. Hedrick, *A History of Horticulture in America to 1860* (New York: Oxford University Press, 1950), 163.

20. Hedrick, *A History of Horticulture* (1950), 81.

CHAPTER 3

1. Quoted in Michael Williams, *Americans and Their Forests: A Historical Geography* (Cambridge, UK: Cambridge University Press, 1992), 253.

2. Christopher Davies, "Life at the Edge: Urban and Industrial Evolution of Texas, Frontier Wilderness—Frontier Space, 1836–1986," *Southwestern Historical Quarterly* 89, no. 4 (April 1986): 443–554.

3. Vera Lea Dugas, "Texas Industry, 1860–1880," *Southwestern Historical Quarterly* 59, no. 2 (October 1955): 172.

4. Williams, *Americans and Their Forests*, 240–250.

5. Robin W. Doughty, "Settlement and Environmental Change in Texas, 1820–1900," *Southwestern Historical Quarterly* 89, no. 4 (April 1986): 424, 429; also see Mark Cowell, "Presettlement Piedmont Forests: Patterns of Composition and Disturbance in Central Georgia," *Annals of the Association of American Geographers* 85, no. 1 (March 1995): 61–83.

6. "From Texas," *Freeman and Messenger*, November 17, 1940, newspaperarchive.com, accessed March 24, 2011.

7. W. Kendall, "Texas," *New York Times*, October 13, 1858; Davies, "Life at the Edge," 451.

8. *Arkansas Daily Gazette*, July 15, 1875.

9. Ibid.

10. Clarence Arthur Reed, *The Pecan* (Washington, DC: U.S. Government Printing Office, 1913), 12.

11. *Arkansas Daily Gazette*, July 15, 1875.

12. Walter B. Stevens, *Through Texas: A Series of Interesting Letters* (St. Louis, MO: St. Louis Southwestern Railway, 1892), 90.

13. Ibid.; Terry Cae, "Pecans and Cotton," *Dallas Morning News*, October 10, 1889.

14. William Keith Guthrie, "Flood Alley: An Environmental History of Flooding in Texas" (PhD diss., University of Kansas), 13.

15. Stuart Pecan Company, "The Pecan and How to Grow It" (Chicago: Women's Temperance Publishing Association, 1893), 18; "Pecans Profiting Oklahoma Farms," *Christian Science Monitor*, December 26, 1925, 5B; Flack, "The Spread and Domestication of the Pecan," 20.

16. *Aurora and Franklin Gazette*, February 18, 1825; *Rhode Island American*, December 3, 1818; *Galveston News*, January 8, 1874; *Arkansas Democrat*, August 26, 1899.

17. Amos Andrew Parker, *Trip to the West and Texas* (Concord, NH: William White, 1835), 176; Oran M. Roberts, *A Description of Texas: Its Advantages and Resources* (St. Louis, MO: Gilbert Book Company, 1881),

31; "Pecans, North," *San Antonio Express*, November 18, 1873, 3; *Texas Almanac and State Industrial Guide* (Dallas: Belo and Company, 1904), accessed through Google eBooks.

18. *Milwaukee Sentinel*, "Hard Times in Texas," October 14, 1842; Stevens, *Through Texas*, 90; *The Missionary Chronicle* (Presbyterian Church in the U.S.A., 1847).

19. Reed, *The Pecan*, 22.

20. Corsa, *Nut Culture in the United States*, 53; Charles Sealsfield, *The Cabin Book, or Sketches of Lives in Texas* (London: J. Winchester, 1844), chapter 3; Walter B. Stevens, "Letter from Texas," *Carroll County Times*, March 23, 1877.

21. "Tree Planting," *Daily Gazette*, September 28, 1869; *St. Louis Inquirer*, June 2, 1819; Kendall, "Texas"; Jeff Ball, "The Tasty Pecan," 46; Clint Crowe, *War in the Nations: The Devastation of a Removed People during the American Civil War* (PhD diss., University of Arkansas-Fayetteville, 2004).

22. "Girl Picks Nuts by Balloon," *New York Times*, November 9, 1902.

23. "Siftings," *Galveston News*, October 23, 1880; "Pecans," *San Antonio Express*, November 9, 1869; ibid., November 27, 1869; "Thieves at Work," *Times Picayune*, October 17, 1886; Sealsfield, *The Cabin Book*; "Pecans," *Houston Telegraph*, October 12, 1848.

24. "Pecan Industry," *The Handbook of Texas Online* (Austin: Texas State Historical Association), http://www.tshaonline.org/handbook/online/articles/dip02.

25. "Savannah Grows Pecans," *Charleston Mercury*, November 7, 1856; *San Antonio Express*, November 2, 1867; ibid., October 29, 1969; *Times Picayune*, December 3, 1865; *San Antonio Express*, October 30, 1867; *San Francisco Bulletin*, November 23, 1869; *San Antonio Express*, November 12, 1869; *Columbia Daily Enquirer*, December 20, 1877; *San Antonio Express*, November 13, 1970; ibid., December 6, 1870; *Dallas Morning News*, October 17, 1889.

26. Luther Burbank, *How Plants Are Trained to Work for Man*, vol. 8 (New York: Fifi Collier and Son, 1914), 20.

CHAPTER 4

1. Christopher Thacker, The History of Gardens (Berkeley: University of California Press, 1985), 57; John Geissler, *The New Oxford Book of Food Plants* (Oxford: Oxford University Press, 2009), 82.

2. Kingsbury, *Hybrid*, 25.

3. Ken Mudge, Jules Janick, Steven Scofield, and Elienzer E. Gold-schmidt, "A History of Grafting," *Horticultural Reviews* 35 (2009): 439.

4. Ibid.

5. F. W. Brison, *American Nut Journal* (September 1923): 52.

6. http://fcit.usf.edu/florida/docs/p/pecan2.htm.

7. F. W. Brison, "Variations in Pecans," *Journal of Heredity* 13, no. 8 (1922), in "pecan excerpts" file.

8. Aaron de Groft, "Eloquent Vessels/Poetics of Power: The Heroic Stoneware of 'Dave the Potter,'" *Winterthur Portfolio* 33, no. 4 (Winter 1988): 249–260.

9. http://aggie-horticulture.tamu.edu/CARYA/pecans/Centennial .HTM

10. http://extension.missouri.edu/publications/DisplayPub.aspx?P=G6971. Thomas Fessenden, *The Complete Farmer and Rural Economist* (New York: C. M. Saxton, 1851), 147.

11. R. B. Hayes and Guy M. Bryan, "The Bryan-Hayes Correspondence, XVII," *Southwestern Historical Quarterly* 19, no. 2 (October 1925): 151–156.

12. Ibid., 151; "Death of Abner Landrum," *Charleston Courier*, April 7, 1859; Charlotte Cassels, "Pottery Works Are Art Form," *Aiken Standard*, October 5, 1978, 8; de Groft, "Eloquent Vessels/Poetics of Power."

13. http://aggie-horticulture.tamu.edu/CARYA/pecans/Centennial .HTM.

14. Works Project Administration, *Slave Narratives: A Folk History of Slavery in the United States*, released October 5, 2004, www.gutenberg.org /files/13602/13602-h/13602-h.htm, accessed April 20, 2011.

15. W. A. Taylor, "Promising New Fruits," in *Yearbook of the Department of Agriculture*, ed. George William Hall (Washington, DC: U.S. Government Printing Office, 1904).

16. "Death of Hubert Bonzano," *Times Picayune*, February 1, 1891.

17. *Yearbook of the Usda, 1904* (Washington, DC: U.S. Government Printing Office, 1905), 406.

18. "Richard Frotscher: Death of the Leading Horticulturalist and Useful Citizen," *Daily Picayune*, February 3, 1986.

19. H. Harold Hume, *The Pecan and Its Culture* (published by author, 1910), 138.

20. Corsa, *Nut Culture in the United States*, 50.

21. Ibid., 52.

22. Reed, *The Pecan*, 12.

23. Ibid., 20. The general topic of scientific farming, and its so-

cial implications, has a rich historiography. One should consult the following books for an overview: Benjamin R. Cohen, *Notes from the Ground: Science, Soil, and Society in the American Countryside* (New Haven, CT: Yale University Press, 2011); Steven Stoll, *Larding the Lean Earth: Soil and Society in Nineteenth-Century America* (New York: Hill and Wang, 2003); and Philip J. Pauly, *Fruits and Plains: The Horticultural Transformation of America* (Cambridge, MA: Harvard University Press, 2008).

24. F. M. Burnette, William Carter Stubbs, and Harcourt Alexander Morgan, *Pecans* (Louisiana State Board of Agriculture, 1902), 851.

25. "California Booms Pecan Industry," *Christian Science Monitor*, October 16, 1922.

26. "Industrial Notes," *Daily Evening Bulletin*, June 30, 1868; "Tree Planting in Our Valleys," *Daily Evening Bulletin*, September 29, 1869; "Budding Pecans upon the Hickory," *New Orleans Times*, May 9, 1875; Isabel K. Billings, "Pecan Industry in the United States," *Economic Geography* 22, no. 3 (1946): 220.

27. "Pecans and English Walnuts," *Macon Telegraph*, October 7, 1887; "Pecans in Georgia," *Macon Telegraph*, October 24, 1886.

28. Corsa, *Nut Culture in the United States*, 51, 53.

29. Max Planck, *Scientific Autobiography and Other Papers* (Philosophical Library, 1968), 34.

30. Corsa, *Nut Culture in the United States*, 54.

31. "The Pecan Tree and Nut," *Daily Gazette*, March 25, 1870; "Nut Trees for Shade," *Hinds County Gazette*, February 8, 1872; "Plant Trees," *Daily Gazette*, January 28, 1874; "Savannah Grown Pecans," November 5, 1875; Corsa, *Nut Culture in the United States*, 50. As late as 1902 a popular publication on the nation's pecan cultivation could report as a matter of fact that "all of the older pecan groves are seedlings"; Burnette et al., *Pecans*, 852.

32. Elmer L. Callihan, "Texas Is Going Nutty," *Texas Monthly* 5, no. 4 (1930): 432.

33. Corsa, *Nut Culture in the United States*, 57.

CHAPTER 5

1. National Pecan Growers Association, *Report of the Proceedings of the Annual Convention of the National Pecan Growers Association* (Author, 1926), 91.

2. Burnette et al., *Pecans*, 851.

3. George W. Oliver, *Budding the Pecan* (Washington, DC: U.S. Government Printing Office, 1902), 10.

4. G. M. Bacon, *Illustrated Catalogue And Price-list Of Grafted, Budded And Choice Seedling Papershell Pecans And Other Nut-bearing Trees: With A Treatise On Pecan Culture* (self-published, 1902), 17.

5. Corsa, *Nut Culture in the United States*, 55.

6. Ibid., 56.

7. Ibid.

8. Callihan, "Texas Is Going Nutty," 433.

9. Ibid., 435–441.

10. Clarence Arthur Reed, *Pecan Culture: With Special Reference to Propagation and Varieties* (USDA, 1916), 8.

11. James E. McWilliams, *American Pests: America's War on Insects from Colonial Times to DDT* (New York: Columbia University Press, 2008), 95–96.

12. Ibid., 40–45.

13. Ibid.

14. Bacon, *Illustrated Catalogue*, 6.

15. M. R. Osborn, *Insects and Diseases of the Pecan and Their Control*, USDA Bulletin 1829: 1940 (Washington, DC: USDA, 1954).

16. Ibid.

17. Callihan, "Texas Is Going Nutty," 441.

18. James Gieson, *Boll Weevil Blues* (Athens: University of Georgia Press, 2011).

19. Callihan, "Texas Is Going Nutty," 441; F. W. Brison, "The Pecan Crop," *Journal of Heredity* 13 (1922): 5.

20. E. E. Risien, "Eastern v. Western Pecans," *Bulletin of the Texas Department of Agriculture* 8 (1909); Corsa, *Nut Culture in the United States*, 58.

21. "The Improved Pecan," *McIntosh County Democrat*, July 21, 1927.

22. "Texas Farm News," *Texas Monthly*.

23. "Interest in Pecan Culture Increases," *Los Angeles Times*, April 22, 1920; "Arizona Man Finds Pecans Good 'Game,'" *Los Angeles Times*, August 5, 1928; "South Carolina Harvests Pecans," *Christian Science Monitor*, November 11, 1932.

24. *Pecan and Its Culture*, 12; Bacon, *Illustrated Catalogue*, 15.

25. H. A. Halrert, "The Edible Nuts of Texas," *Texas Almanac and State Industrial Guide* 8 (1904): 6.

26. Helen King, "Haven't We a Place for the Pecan?" *Los Angeles Times*, August 4, 1929.

27. National Pecan Growers Association, *Report*, 83.

CHAPTER 6

1. Paul K. Conkin, *A Revolution Down on the Farm: The Transformation of American Agriculture since 1929* (Louisville: University Press of Kentucky, 2009).

2. William Henry Chandler, *North American Orchards* (Philadelphia: Lea and Febiger, 1928), 12.

3. H. P. Stuckey and Edwin Jackson Kyle, *Pecan Growing* (New York: The Macmillan Company, 1925), 51–57.

4. Ibid., 55–60.

5. Ibid., 108–109.

6. National Pecan Growers Association, *Report of the Proceedings of the Annual Convention of the National Pecan Growers Association* (Author, 1926), 139.

7. Stuckey and Kyle, *Pecan Growing*, 112.

8. Ibid.

9. Ibid., 116; "Pecans," *Los Angeles Times*, February 22, 1931, and April 12, 1931.

10. Manaster, *Pecans*, 24; Jane Manaster, *The Pecan Tree* (Austin: University of Texas Press, 1995).

11. Robert Tomsho, "Pecan Industry Finds Getting Organized Is Driving It Nuts," *Wall Street Journal*, April 1, 1994.

12. Manaster, *Pecans*, 50.

13. National Pecan Growers Association, *Report*, 112.

14. Ibid., 120–122, 144.

15. Ibid.

16. *New York Times*, December 19, 1942; *Christian Science Monitor*, November 29, 1938; *New York Times*, October 12, 1937; *New York Times*, July 22, 1939; *Wall Street Journal*, October 28, 1937.

17. *Los Angeles Times*, April 12, 1931.

18. Kenneth P. Walker, "The Pecan Shellers of San Antonio and Mechanization," *Southwestern Historical Quarterly* 69, no. 1 (1965).

19. Jules V. Powell and Donn A. Reimund, *The Pecan Shelling and Processing Industry: Practices, Problems, Prospects*, USDA Economic Research Service, Agriculture Economic Report 15 (September 1962): 1–3.

CHAPTER 7

1. "Nuts Urged as Food," *New York Times*, November 9, 1942; "Pecan Prices Decline," *Wall Street Journal*, November 24, 1948; Jane Nickerson,

"News of Food," *New York Times*, December 1, 1948; "News of Food," *New York Times*, November 20, 1949; "Government to Buy Pecans," *New York Times*, November 21, 1951.

2. Jane Holt, "News of Food," *New York Times*, November 11, 1942.

3. Jane Nickerson, *New York Times*, "News of Food," November 8, 1945; Mary Meade, "Carrot Pecan Loaf," *Chicago Daily Tribune*, August 9, 1954; "News of Food," *New York Times*, November 30, 1946; "Nuts Urged as Food," *New York Times*, November 9, 1942, 36; Jane Nickerson, "News of Food," *New York Times*, October 6, 1948.

4. "Ceilings for Nutmeats," *New York Times*, October 31, 1943; "Pecan Prices Decline," *Wall Street Journal*, November 24, 1948; "Schools Asked for Pecans," *Chicago Daily Tribune*, March 23, 1952; "US Spends $1,287,600 to Support Pecan Prices," *New York Times*, January 5, 1952.

5. Mary Meade, "Pecans Popular in Sandwiches or Tasty Desserts," *Chicago Daily Tribune*, December 28, 1947.

6. Mary Meade, "Cheaper Nuts," *Chicago Daily Tribune*, February 21, 1936; Mary Meade, "Pecan Drops in Price for Use of Budgeteers," *Chicago Daily Tribune*, January 9, 1936.

7. Jane Holt, "News of Food," *New York Times*, May 13, 1942; Mary Meade, "How to Make New Orleans' Pecan Pralines," *Chicago Daily Tribune*, November 1, 1947.

8. Clementine Paddleford, "Atlanta: Georgia Pecan Pie," *Los Angeles Times*, July 7, 1949.

9. "Orange Pecan Pie Wins Recipe Prize," *Washington Post*, September 12, 1931; "Louisiana Yam Pecan Pie," *Washington Post and Times Herald*, February 6, 1959; "New Nut Recipes," *Washington Post*, November 18, 1938.

10. Jane Holt, "News of Food," *New York Times*, November 11, 1942; Mary Meade, "Pecans Popular in Sandwiches," *Chicago Daily Tribune*, December 28, 1947; Marian Manners, "Pecan Biscuits Presented for Culinary Trial," *Los Angeles Times*, July 18, 1939.

11. Jane Holt, "News of Food," November 24, 1948; "Nuts to Be Plentiful," *New York Times*, October 3, 1946.

12. Florence Brobeck, "Fresh Nuts for Holiday Tables," *New York Times*, November 8, 1936; Helen Van Pelt Wilson, "Most Useful Nut Trees," *New York Times*, February 14, 1943; *New York Times*, November 11, 1943.

13. Campos de Moura, "Experimental Vitamin A Deficiency; Action of Pecan Oil," *Anais da Faculdade de Medicina da Universidade de São Paolo* 14 (1938): 185–212; H. Levine, "The Pecan Nut as a Source of Vitamin

A," *Journal of Home Economics* 24 (1932): 49–53; R. B. French, Ovida Davis Abbott, and Ruth O. Townsend, "Levels of Thiamine, Riboflavin, and Niacin in Florida-Produced Foods," Bulletin 482, University of Florida Experiment Stations, August 1951; Cary Blake, "New Mexico Tops in Pecans," *Southwest Farm Press*, May 3, 2007.

14. "News of Food," *New York Times*, November 24, 1948; Jane Nickerson, "Food: Storage of Pecans," *New York Times*, December 29, 1956.

15. "News of Food," *New York Times*, November 29, 1950; ibid., *New York Times*, April 13, 1959.

16. http://inventors.about.com/library/inventors/blfrfood.htm, accessed December 11; Gordon Follette, "Frozen Foods: The Formative Years. 100 Years of Refrigeration," supplement to *ASHRAE Journal* 46 (November 2004): S35–S39; June Owen, "Food: New Products," *New York Times*, March 23, 1959.

17. Lois Baker, "Round the Food Stores," *Chicago Daily Tribune*, September 17, 1965; "New Food Products," *Washington Post*, December 4, 1969; Obituary, "William Stuckey, 67; Built Candy Store into National Chain," *New York Times*, January 8, 1977.

18. http://www.library.hbs.edu/hc/lehman/chrono.html?company=standard_brands_incorporated; "Standard Brands Acquires Southern Pecan Shelling," *Wall Street Journal*, September 30, 1954; http://en.wikipedia.org/wiki/Pet,_Inc.#History; "Pet Milk Processing Plant," *Wall Street Journal*, March 12, 1963; "Retail Entrepreneurs of the Year: J. Givens Young," *Chain Store Age* 73, no. 12 (December 1997): 114.

19. "To Make Good Food," *Washington Post*, October 7, 1900; Mary Meade, "Tasty Recipes Lend Variety to Lenten Meal," *Chicago Daily Tribune*, February 22, 1933, 19; Phyllis Hanes, "'Natural' Cereals—How to Produce Your Own," *Christian Science Monitor*, February 21, 1974; "More Bounce to the Ounce," *New York Times*, December 7, 1952.

20. Ruth Casa-Emellos, "The All-Round Pecan," *New York Times*, January 10, 1954.

21. "Ice Cream Processing and Packaging," *Dairy Foods*, October 1996, 37; "Today's Ice Cream Flavors: More than Neapolitan," *Dairy Foods*, October 1996, 97.

22. Betsy Spethmann, *Brandweek* 36 (August 7, 1995): 26; "The Wizard of Oats," *Consumer Reports*, October 1996, 61.

23. John Mariant, "Pecan Pie," *Restaurant Hospitality*, December 1998, 12.

24. "It's the Year of Plenty for Pecans," *Christian Science Monitor*, October 26, 1965, 4; Pamela Parseghian, "Enchiladas on a Roll," *Nation's*

Restaurant News 28 (August 1, 1994): 75; Alan Liddle, "Birnbaum Goes Solo," *Nation's Restaurant News* 28 (May 9, 1994): 3; Susanne Hall, "Georgia on Her Mind," *Restaurants and Institutions* (October 1, 1996): 23; "The Recipes," *Restaurant Business* (October 1, 1997): 138–141.

CHAPTER 8

1. http://horttech.ashspublications.org/content/5/3/202.full.pdf.

2. Tomsho, "Pecan Industry."

3. John Huey, "Pecan Growers See Bigger '75 Harvest," *Wall Street Journal*, December 26, 1975.

4. Ibid.

5. Ibid. Description from F. W. Williams, M. G. Laplante, and E. K. Heaton, "The Consumer Market for Pecans and Competing Nuts," *Southern Journal of Agricultural Economics* (July 1972): 104.

6. Chad Dorn, "Nut Marketing Going Nutty in 96," *Candy Industry* (October 1996): 33–34; Doyle C. Johnson, "Economic Trends in the U.S. Pecan Market," *ERS-USDA* (March 1998): 21; Tomsho, "Pecan Industry."

7. Izchukwu M. Onunkwo and James E. Epperson, "Export Demand for U.S. Pecans: Impact of U.S. Export Promotion Programs" (paper presented at the annual meeting of the Agricultural Economics Association, Nashville, Tennessee, August 8–11, 1999); Johnson, "Economic Trends in the U.S. Pecan Market."

8. Guojin Sun, "An International Trade Analysis of the Impact of the North American Free Trade Agreement on U.S. Pecan Producers" (PhD diss., University of Georgia, 1991), 3–4; Janet Jacobs, "Japanese Market Tough Nut to Crack," *Corsicana Daily Sun*, December 9, 2006.

9. "China Buys $4.5 million Worth of NM Pecan Crop," *Lubbock Online*, March 25, 2007; "Jeff Worn Says Pecan Exports Threaten Domestic Consumption," *Growing Georgia* (October 13, 2010), accessed online at http://growinggeorgia.com.

10. Lourdes Medrano, "China Goes Nuts over Pecans," *Fiscal Times*, January 4, 2012; David Wessel, "Shell Shock: Chinese Demand Reshapes U.S. Pecan Business," *Wall Street Journal*, April 18, 2011, accessed January 18, 2012.

11. Jill Galus, "New Mexico Pecans Driving China Nuts" (transcript of KVIA report, Las Cruces, New Mexico, November 15, 2010); Wessel, "Shell Shock."

12. Jennifer Paire, "Pecan Growers Go Global," *Growing Magazine*, May 2011 (online edition).

13. http://www.boston.com/news/nation/articles/2011/11/07/drought _demand_from_china_drive_up_pecan_prices/; Shlachter, "Texas Has High Demand but Not Enough Pecans," *Fort Worth Star-Telegram*, October 9, 2011, accessed online at www.star-telegram.com/2011/10/29 /v-touch/3483226/texas-has-high-demand-but-not.html.

14. Josephine Bennett, "Georgia Farmers Hail China's New Taste for Pecans," NPR, July 7, 2011.

15. William D. Goff, "Commercial Pecan Insect and Disease Control" (Extension Pecan Specialist, Auburn University, 2011).

16. http://pecankernel.tamu.edu/pecan_insects/pests/index.html; http://extension.missouri.edu/p/mp711.

17. http://www.caes.uga.edu/commodities/fruits/pecan/growers /documents/pecan%20fungicide.pdf.

BIBLIOGRAPHIC ESSAY

As far as general works go, the only pre-existing single volume on the pecan tree's history is Jane Manaster's excellent *Pecans: The Story in a Nutshell* (Austin: University of Texas Press, 1994; republished by Texas Tech University Press in 2008). The book provides a concise overview of the pecan's pivotal developments, especially when it comes to the emergence of different cultivars and the stories of the breeders behind them. Manaster's work fits nicely in the context of several broader histories of plant breeding, including Noel Kingsbury's comprehensive *Hybrid: The History and Science of Plant Breeding* (Chicago: University of Chicago Press, 2011), Jonathan Silvertown's *An Orchard Invisible: A Natural History of Seeds* (Chicago: University of Chicago Press, 2010), and Jane S. Smith's *The Garden of Invention: Luther Burbank and the Business of Breeding Plants* (New York: Penguin, 2010). Luther Burbank's papers themselves also proved invaluable to me for understanding the process of plant breeding.

Information on the interactions of Indians, Europeans, and pecans was gleaned from a wider range of sources, including *The Indians of Texas* by W. W. Newcomb, Jr. (Austin: The University of Texas Press, 1961), Paul A. Delcourt and Hazel R. Delcourt's *Prehistoric Native Americans and Ecological Change: Human Ecosystems in Eastern North America since the Pleistocene* (Cambridge, UK: Cambridge University Press, 2004); and Jean Richardson Flack's 1970 University of Wisconsin dissertation, "The Spread and Domestication of the Pecan (*Carya illinoensis*) in the United States." My analysis of the ecological relationships between pecans and non-human animals was deeply informed by articles in the journals *Botanical Review*, *Journal of Mammalogy*, and *Wilson Bulletin*. The big picture of bioprospecting was framed by Londa Schiebinger's *Plants and Empire: Colonial Bioprospecting in the Atlantic World* (Cambridge, MA: Harvard University Press, 2004). The best source I know of for information on the European encounter with the pecan comes from Rodney Howard True, "Notes on the Early History of the Pecan in America," in the *Annual Report of the Board of Regents* (1919) of the Smithsonian Institution.

Histories of scientific agriculture, grafting, and plant breeding are numerous in the field of American environmental history. I relied primarily on Philip J. Pauly's *Fruits and Plains: The Horticultural Transformation of America* (Cambridge, MA: Harvard University Press, 2008), Benjamin

R. Cohen's *Notes from the Ground: Science, Soil, and Society in the American Coun-*
tryside (New Haven: Yale University Press, 2011), Deborah Fitzgerald's
Every Farm a Factory: The Industrial Ideal in American Agriculture (New Haven: Yale
University Press, 2010), and Steven Stoll's *Larding the Lean Earth: Soil and*
Society in Nineteenth-Century America (New York: Hill and Wang, 2003).
These are all critical works in their fields. For information on the
actual logistics of grafting and plantation building, it helps to go back
to the sources from that time. See H. P. Stuckey and Edwin Jackson
Kyle, *Pecan Growing* (New York: The MacMillan Company, 1925) and
Clarence Arthur Reed, *Pecan Culture: With Special Reference to Propagation and*
Varieties (USDA, 1916).

I relied on several general sources for background on deforestation,
Indians, and Anglo migration into western regions. See Michael Wil-
liams's magisterial *Americans and Their Forests: A Historical Geography* (Cambridge,
UK: Cambridge University Press, 1992); Lynn A. Nelson's *Pharsalia:*
An Environmental Biography of a Southern Plantation, 1780–1880 (Athens, GA:
University of Georgia Press, 2009); and Charles Hudson and Carmen
Chaves Tesser (eds.), *The Forgotten Centuries: Indians and Europeans in the American*
South, 1521–1704 (Athens, GA: University of Georgia Press, 1994).

Telling the story of a single commodity presents the ongoing challenge of context—as in, how much or how little to provide. I relied on
several histories of single crops as models for how to handle the context
issue. These included Larry Zuckerman's *The Potato: How the Humble Spud*
Rescued the Western World (New York: North Point Press, 1999) and Pierre
Laszlo's *Salt: Grain of Life* (New York: Ecco Press, 2002). Other notable
examples of well-balanced commodity books are Arthur Allen's *Ripe:*
The Search for the Perfect Tomato (New York: Counterpoint, 2011) and Dan
Koeppel's *Banana: The Fate of the Fruit That Changed the World* (New York: Plume,
2008).

To the extent that the pecan's story is the story of industrialization,
there are several excellent works that helped me frame the pecan's
path toward globalization. See Alan Olmstead's and Paul W. Rhode's
Creating Abundance: Biological Innovation and American Agricultural Development
(Cambridge, UK: Cambridge University Press, 2008) and Paul K.
Conkin's *A Revolution Down on the Farm: The Transformation of American Agriculture*
since 1929 (Louisville: University of Kentucky Press, 2009) for two superb
histories of industrial agriculture. An excellent complement to these
volumes was a plethora of trade magazines highlighting the marketing
and consumption of pecans. Particularly notable was *Nation's Restaurant*
News, which highlighted key culinary trends involving the pecan.

Index

Florida, 55, 57–58, 70, 77, 84–86, 93–94, 107, 125–126
French explorers, 24–26
frontier, 26, 34, 41–42, 44, 48, 61
Frotscher, Richard, 65–67, 69
fungicides, 135, 149

genes. *See* diversity, genetic
Georgia: early pecan growing in, 61, 70–71, 77, 78, 80, 93–96; modern pecan industry in, 20, 55, 92, 96, 115, 129, 133, 144; peaches, 53; pecan pie, 122, 128
Girardeau, J. H., 86
Gordon, W. W., 71
grafting, 51, 52, 56, 57, 58, 59, 65–67, 70, 79, 84, 86; bark, 103; chip, 102–103; cleft, 84, 86; tongue, 84; and USDA, 89–90; wax, 86, 102, wedge, 84; whip, 84
Guthrie, William Keith, 38

Halbert, Herbert, 107–108
Hall, Grant, 17
Hamilton, William, 28
Hayes, Rutherford B., 57
herbicides, 135, 147, 148
hickory, 3, 145
Holt, Jane, 125
Hong Kong, 141
horticulture, 65, 57
Howard, N. B., 84
Hume, Harold, 96

Illinois, 3–4, 15, 17, 25, 37
immigrants, German, 46, 63, 65, 75

India, 53–54, 146, 154
Indians. *See* Native Americans
industrialization, 34, 112, 115, 147, 172
insecticides, 88–89, 92, 93, 147
insects, 9, 15, 55, 82, 86, 88, 91–93, 100, 104, 136, 138, 147–150, 154. *See also* pecan pests
integrated pest management, 136, 147, 148
intercropping, 104, 105, 106
irrigation, 2, 52, 68, 69, 150

Japan, 141
Jefferson, Thomas, 28–31, 155
Jim Crow, 109
Juglandaceae, 3, 20
Juglans Pacane, 28

Karo Corn Syrup, 121, 132
Keller, John, 83
Kendall, G. W., 35, 45
Kentucky, 37, 84
Kline, John G., 84
Klingeman, Emma B., 86–87

labor, 7–8, 16, 44, 62, 68–70, 75, 81, 85, 101, 104, 113, 138, 150
Landrum, Abner, 58–61, 88
logging, 32–34
Louisiana, 4, 8, 17, 32–33, 37–39, 42–44, 50, 61, 63, 71, 72, 78, 146. *See also* New Orleans

mail-order, 126–127
Manifest Destiny, 35, 42
market (for pecans), 39, 40,

47–48, 55, 60, 98, 116,
136–138, 141
marketing, III, 116, 141
Marshall, Humphry, 28
masting, ix, 8, 9, 18, 47, 105,
110, 111, 139; and pigs, 41
Meade, Mary, 120
Mexico, 4, 20, 93, 136, 141
Millicent, Elsie, 132
Mississippi (state), 4, 8, 37,
61–63, 73, 77, 83, 106
Mississippi River, 5, 11, 24, 26,
36, 61, 74
monoculture, 38, 99, 147
mutualism, 14, 18

National Pecan Growers Association, 108, 109
National Pecan Marketing Association, 112
Native Americans, x, *xvi*, 5, 7–11,
12, 13, 14–17, 18, 19, 23–26,
33, 35, 41, 42, 54, 126,
158n7
natural control, 15, 16
New Mexico, 10, 55, 109, 136;
as modern pecan producer,
20, 93, 142–143
New Orleans, 26, 39–40, 47–
48, 61, 65, 74, 83, 106–107,
113, 120–121
New York, 26, 28, 71, 96, 119,
126
Nickerson, Jane, 117
Norfleet, Lizzie, 62
Nueces River, 11, 25
nursery business, 27, 67, 74–75,
78–79, 80–81, 87, 90, 95,
101, 107, 109, 136

Ohio River Valley, 26, 27
Oklahoma, 4, 17, 39, 109, 113
Oliver, George W., 79

Pacane, *xvi*
Parker, A. A., 40
peach, 19, 51, 53–54, 56, 64
pecan farming, 100, 110, 135,
147–150; commercial, 20,
56, 61, 72, 92, 100–106,
163–164n23; density, 103;
economics, 98; intercrop-
ping, 105–106; regions, 109;
startup costs of, 68; subsidies, III, 117–118. *See also* cultivation, passive; USDA
pecan nut: as commodity, 39,
140; harvest techniques, 6,
45; kernel, 27, 48–49, 64,
138; mail-order, 126–127;
marketing, 112, 115–117,
124, 140; meal, 8; as meat
substitute, 16–17, 117, 125,
129, 158n3; nutritional val-
ues, 7, 17, 18, 124, 125, 144,
158n3; oil, 129; pie, 116,
119, 120–124, 127–128, 132,
139, 145; poaching, 45, 150;
polished, 40; pralines, 26,
199, 121; preparation, 8, 24;
recipes, 18, 116–117, 118, 119,
120–124, 127, 129; in school
lunches, 118; shell, 1–2, 7, 17,
129, 133; storage, 16–17, 127;
surplus, 134. *See also* cultivars,
pecan
pecan pests: aphid, 148; Asian
ambrosia beetle, 148; fall
webworm, 92, 148; fire ant,
148; pecan budmoth, 92;

pecan leaf casebearer, 92; pecan nut casebearer, 91, 148; pecan phylloxera, 148; pecan weevil, 92, 148; soldier bugs, 86; spider mite, 148; spittlebug, 92, 148; stinkbug, 148; walnut caterpillar, 148; wood lice, 86; yellow aphid, 154. *See also* crows; raccoons; squirrels; wood rats

pecan tree (Carya illinoiensis): as climax species, 3; as commodity, 30, 109, 136; disease resistance, 107, 152; diseases, 104, 149; failure to "come true," 57, 60, 72, 79; felling for nuts, 36–37, 42; native range, 3, 68; passive cultivation, 33, 38, 42–48, 54, 73, 74, 79, 81, 91, 94, 101; pollination, 4; root system, 4, 94, 103, 104; wild, 33, 37–38, 75, 81, 147, 152–153; yield, 36, 43–44, 48, 51, 69–70, 75, 78, 81, 84, 94, 105, 107, 110–111. *See also* cultivars, pecan; genetic diversity; grafting

pecan wood, 22; cabinetry, 23; drying methods, 22–23; flooring, 23, 130; furniture, 23; market, 130; trim, 23

pest control, 52, 89–91, 92, 148, 149

pesticide, 92, 99, 133, 135, 138, 154

pig farming, 40–41

pine, 18, 32–34, 42

Planck, Max, 72

plum, 57, 64

Pollan, Michael, 130, 157n3

Pope, J. D., 97

Prince, William, 27

protein, 7, 117, 125, 129, 158

Prudhomme, Paul, 133

Pyles, Stephan, 133

raccoons, 15, 150

railroads, 31

Reed, C. A., 109

resistance: to disease, 152; to pesticides, 149, 154

Risien, Edmond E., 83, 34, 94, 107, 132

Roberts, Oran, 41

Roman, Telesphore J., 61–62

Roosevelt, Eleanor, 124

Roosevelt, Franklin D., 113

rooting, of figs, olives, and pomegranates, 57

San Antonio, Texas, 39, 46–47, 48, 113

San Saba, Texas, 74, 83, 107, 132, 140

Scott, Willard, 137

shelling machines, 111, 113

slavery, 60, 61; and passive pecan cultivation, 61–62

Snow, Charles Henry, 22

soil: alluvial, 3; enhancement, 52; quality, 95, 103

South Carolina, 53, 55, 60, 93, 96

Southern Pecan Shelling Company, 113, 128

Spanish explorers, 10, 19, 24

sprayers, 92, 99

squirrels, 11–12, 14, 17, 150

Standard Brands, 128, 129